The Legacy of Monsignor James Kirwin (1872-1926)

Sr. Madeleine Grace, CVI, Ph.D.

En Route Books and Media, LLC
Saint Louis, MO

ENROUTE
Make the time

En Route Books and Media, LLC
5705 Rhodes Avenue
St. Louis, MO 63109

Contact us at
contactus@enroutebooksandmedia.com

Cover Credit: Sebastian Mahfood, using a photo
of Msgr. James Kirwin

ISBN-13: 979-8-88870-548-3
Library of Congress Control Number:
Available online at https://catalog.loc.gov

This Work is Dedicated to

My sister Gretchen Grace

and

My brother John Robert Grace Junior

Table of Contents

Foreword

"Big Jim" Kirwin, otherwise known as Father James M. Kirwin (or Msgr. Kirwin), was the quintessential "man's man" even though a priest. He settled barfights and broke up labor strikes. He instituted martial law after the Galveston storm of 1900. He joined the army as a chaplain and was a major figure in Galveston politics. He was a voice of authority in civil as well as ecclesial matters, and it was he who decided to cremate the bodies of the dead following the Great Storm. There were too many bodies to bury, and the bodies washed up onto the beach after they had been tossed into the Gulf. (Cremation was the only way to dispose of the bodies, and public health required it.) Fr. Kirwin was both a soldier, secular and Christian, and a scholar. He was the rector of a parish, a teacher, the president of a seminary, and a moving orator. He was well-informed about public events and the Church's theology. He had no qualms about speaking out on controversial subjects such as a temperance ordinance or the Ku Klux Klan. He supported the founding of men's groups such as the Catholic students at Texas A&M and the fledgling Knights of Columbus. He exemplified the virtues of the Knights of Columbus: charity, unity, fraternity, and patriotism.

Because of his forthrightness and strength of character, Kirwin suffered at the hands of his enemies. Members of the Klan followed him from Galveston, where he was Chancellor, to St. Mary's Seminary in La Porte, where he was president and instructor, intending to tar and feather him. Most significantly, an anonymous letter was sent to the Vatican reporting that Kirwin did not believe in the

Catholic dogma on the resurrection of the body because he allowed cremation of the bodies left by the storm of 1900. Fr. Kirwin's elevation to monsignor was delayed twenty years because of this.

Fr. Kirwin's life was inextricably entwined with the lives of the bishops and the life of the Galveston Diocese (now Archdiocese of Galveston/Houston). Bishop Nicholas Gallagher engaged Fr. Kirwin to move to the Diocese. He appointed him to do most of the public speaking at Diocesan events since Gallagher was a shy man and not a particularly effective speaker. Kirwin was known to Bishop Gallagher, as he had attended the same seminary while Gallagher was a priest of that diocese. The Galveston Diocese was in turmoil because Bishop Claude Dubuis had retired from the duties of the office of Bishop without retiring from the office itself. Infighting had developed among the faction of priests. Some of the priests were devoted to Bishop Dubuis, mainly those from France, while others were devoted to Fr. Chaland, who was known for his clear-headed thinking. When Bishop Gallagher arrived, his personality did not lend itself to settling the tension, and his first actions upon arriving made the situation worse. Because of the many years of Kirwin's devotion to the good of the diocese, Bishop Christopher Byrne saw in him the same values as Bishop Gallagher had; he continued to depend upon Kirwin after Kirwin's installation as ordinary of Galveston. Kirwin served Bishop Byrne until his own death in 1926.

Despite the number of memorials built to honor Msgr. Kirwin, at his death and closely following, is not as well known as he should be for his service to the diocese during a very volatile period. Kirwin had been such a part of Galveston life that his funeral services lasted four days and stores closed in his honor. Kirwin High School,

Kirwin Memorial, which became the church of the parish of St. Mary's of La Porte, a historical marker, and other physical installations serve as a reminder of his influence. Unfortunately, Kirwin's body was returned to his hometown in Ohio at the request of his mother, and he was buried there.

Sr. Madeleine Grace has become something of an expert on the history of the late 19th/early 20th century of the Diocese of Galveston. She has previously written biographies of Bishop Nicholas Gallagher (Texas A & M Press) and Bishop Christopher Byrne (to be published by En Route Books and Media, LLC). She has built upon the work of such historians as Carlos Castaneda, who wrote a seven-volume history of the Church in Texas, and James Vanderholt, who spent most of his life studying the Church's history in and around Houston. She has also investigated many contemporary newspapers because, although Kirwin has slipped away from the forefront of history, he was a frequent and larger-than-life figure in the daily and Catholic presses.

Dr. Mary Kelleher Fitz, formerly Head Librarian at Beran Library, St. Mary's Seminary, University of St. Thomas School of Theology; formerly Adjunct Professor of English, University of St. Thomas, currently serving as Librarian at Rice University, Houston.

Preface

It is certainly true that one scholarly endeavor can overflow or lead to another. The name of James Kirwin kept coming up within the research I have done on Bishop Nicholas Gallagher and Bishop Christopher Byrne. In fact, Fr. Kirwin could be seen as the glue that became the salvific piece for the episcopate of Bishop Gallagher. After Fr. Kirwin had earned his place within the administration of the Galveston diocese, Bishop Byrne was not about to move him. There he remained, and there he experienced a premature passing. Today, bishops would look again at giving so many tasks to one prelate. At that time, however, two bishops chose to extend his talents far beyond his own for the benefit of the Church.

I am indebted to the individual who served as Archivist for the Catholic Archives of Texas, Marian Barber. She found in her own research in Austin that Msgr. James Kirwin had made substantial contributions in his many roles within the diocese of Galveston. Marian Barber was asking why it took so long for Fr. Kirwin to be made a Monsignor, and why he was never made a Bishop. Then there was a rumor that the Ku Klux Klan wished to tar and feather him. Thus, a committee of Catholics and non-Catholics was formed to prevent that possibility. Msgr. Kirwin was not even a Texan; rather, he was adopted into the Galveston diocese through Bishop Gallagher. It was a significant adoption indeed. At that time, after hearing such comments, I placed his name on the mental reserve shelf, hoping that the opportunity might arise to research his contributions to the Church in the Galveston diocese.

It would have been difficult to forget Msgr. James Kirwin's name, as the anniversary of his death has been commemorated on significant occasions. It is also true that various plaques commemorating his life can be found at the Cathedral of the Sacred Heart in Galveston and at other notable sites. Many students attended Kirwin High School in Galveston. The one hundredth anniversary of Kirwin's passing took place in January, 2026. With these thoughts in mind, the research proceeded.

I am deeply indebted to the following individuals for making this research possible:

Dr. Marian Barber, previous Archivist for the Diocese of Austin and the Catholic Archives of Texas

Sr. Dympna Lyons, CVI, and Sr. Brendan O'Donnell, CVI, Archivists for the Sisters of the Incarnate Word and Blessed Sacrament

Lisa May, Archivist for the Archdiocese of Galveston-Houston

Monsignor James Vanderholt, for his personal research on Msgr. James Kirwin

Bob Giles for his research for the *Texas Catholic Herald*

Msgr. Anton Frank for maintaining an interest among the Catholic War Veterans in Msgr. Kirwin

Selena Aleman, Archivist for the Diocese of Austin and the Catholic Archives of Texas

Dr. Mary Kelleher for proofreading the text and writing the Foreword.

Sr. Theresa Kelleher, CVI, and Sr. Mary Margaret Rosberg, CVI, for proofreading and providing photography for the text.

Chapter One

An Enduring Care for the Diocese of Galveston

When the second Bishop of Galveston, Claude Dubuis, left for France on July 12, 1881, he resigned the administration of the diocese of Galveston, yet retained the title. It appeared he had every intention of going back to his beloved Texas, presuming his own physique would allow it. Such was Claude Dubuis's desire that he appointed those in administrative positions during what he perceived as interim appointments. Dubuis asked the Vatican to appoint a coadjutor bishop as he traveled to France for ongoing medical attention. Pierre Dufal, C.F.C, formerly the Vicar Apostolic of East Bengal, India, was designated as vicar apostolic with the right of succession. The Right Reverend Pierre Dufal arrived in Galveston in 1878. Bishop Dubuis was in France at that time. Fr. Dufal found the priests difficult to deal with. He "struggled vainly to assert his authority." Contention arose between Dufal and Dubuis. Unfortunately, Dufal was not that skilled in English and had difficulty with the climate. Thus, he resigned on April 2, 1879, effective December 9, 1879,[1] and returned to France. Bishop Dubuis made a return and last visit to Texas. He appointed Fr. Theodore Buffard administrator of the diocese and granted power of attorney to Fr. Louis Chaland, the Chancellor. Bishop Dubuis then officially resigned as administrator of the

---

[1] James F. Vanderholt, "Dufal, Pierre," *Handbook of Texas Online.* https://www.tshaonline.org/handbook/entries/dufal-pierre.

diocese on July 12, 1881, but continued to retain the title.[2] Therefore, the jurisdiction of the diocese of Galveston was no longer within his hands.[3]

A Vincentian, A.J. Meyer, who was the current President of St. John the Baptist College in New York City, was then asked to serve as apostolic administrator of the Diocese of Galveston. He asked the diocese to withdraw his name; however, his health was not good. The line of authority within the diocese became confused. Some of the priests took the matter of confusion to Archbishop Napoleon Perche in New Orleans by letter. During this period, Nicholas Gallagher, the Vicar General of the Diocese of Columbus, Ohio, was appointed as the apostolic administrator of the Diocese of Galveston. He had heard of the confusion, especially among the clergy. Bearing that information in mind, he accepted the position as apostolic administrator. He clarified his role by writing all clergy on March 3, 1882, stating that he was taking over jurisdiction of the diocese.[4] He was actually appointed as apostolic administrator of the diocese of Galveston and was made titular archbishop of Canopus from 1882 to 1892. As mentioned earlier, Dubuis did not give up the title of Bishop of Galveston until 1892.[5]

---

[2] Carlos Castañeda, *Our Catholic Heritage in Texas, 1836-1950, v. 7 of Our Catholic Heritage in Texas, 119-1936* (Austin, Texas: Von Boeckmann-Jones, 1958), 478-479.

[3] "History of the Diocese of Galveston-Houston," *Recall, Rejoice, Renew, 1847-1997 Diocese of Galveston-Houston* (Dallas, TX: Taylor Publishing, 1997), 27-28.

[4] Ibid, 30.

[5] Ibid, 30.

Bishop Gallagher had a tall order to fill, in that the position had already been refused by two earlier candidates who had heard about the lack of peace among the clergy on the island. Gallagher was only 36 years old. He would be seen as a "Yankee Bishop" as he rose from above the Mason-Dixon line so soon after the Civil War. Many other prospective bishops may have held out for so-called greener pastures.

Upon taking leadership of the Diocese of Galveston, Bishop Gallagher forbade the Sisters of Charity of the Incarnate Word from seeking postulants in France. He preferred candidates who spoke English rather than French. The Sisters had no contacts in Ireland, so they called upon Bishop Dubuis for help. Bishop Dubuis was not in sufficient health to make the journey to Ireland to recruit. In writing to Bishop Gallagher, Bishop Dubuis offered to send letters of recommendation "to the prelates and high ecclesiastical authorities of Ireland." There is no recorded response from Bishop Gallagher, probably because he did not often save correspondence. As it turned out, no Irish candidates entered the community until the end of the year 1883. This happened not because of planned recruiting. It is thought this was through the industry of the French Sisters. They had begun recruiting English-speaking clergy for the diocese of Galveston, unlike Dubuis, who had obtained priests from France. The Sisters of Charity of the Incarnate Word had for many years recruited Sisters from France. The diocese had been dominated by French-speaking clerics, and this would begin to change.[6]

---

[6] Sr. Loyola Hegarty, *Serving with Gladness, The Origin and History of the Congregation of the Sisters of Charity of the Incarnate Word (Houston,*

When Bishop Gallagher came to preside over the community elections of the Sisters on January 2, 1883, the Sisters were deadlocked for three days. Bishop Gallagher then insisted on Sr. Augustine Edwards as his choice, and she was elected. The records show an almost total exclusion of French Sisters from office. Sr. Augustine Edwards was the first American Superior, having come from San Antonio herself. She had a keen knowledge of the Community's temporal affairs. She spoke with graciousness and humility, which disarmed those who might otherwise have been antagonistic.[7]

The Sisters were further quite disappointed that Bishop Gallagher gave their orphanage in Galveston to the Incarnate Word Sisters in San Antonio to operate. This arrangement remained in effect until 1888, when the Sisters in Galveston were again allowed to operate the orphanage as their membership had grown. Five Irish Sisters had entered between November 1883 and September 1884. Further, Mother M. Augustine went to Canada on a recruiting trip, bringing back seven Canadians and two Irish candidates. All these young women would remain in the fold, save one.[8]

Why had this new bishop chosen English among those he wished to serve when French had been the predominant tongue for some time? Bishop Gallagher had a strong desire to build a native clergy, even though many parishes had parishioners for whom English was a second language, often a poor one.

Texas: Bruce Publishing Co., in Cooperation with the Sisters of Charity of the Incarnate Word, Houston, Texas, 1967), 321-322.

[7] Hegarty, *Serving with Gladness*, 282.

[8] Hegarty, *Serving with Gladness*, 285.

Over time, some parishioners wrote to members of the hierarchy, complaining about certain practices Bishop Gallagher had introduced in the Galveston diocese. One was the closing of the Ursuline convent in Galveston to visitors. Catholics had attended Mass there for many years. These Sisters had deep roots in Galveston, dating back to before the Civil War. In fact, the Sisters helped the city through the War. Bishop Gallagher believed these parishioners should attend their own parish churches and support those parishes financially.

Some Catholics believed that the way Bishop Gallagher treated parishioners was offensive. Further, if parishioners loved a priest, they knew they would lose him. They further believed that the Bishop's unkindness toward some of the priests had driven them away. The Bishop was accused of giving preferential treatment to the Dominican Sisters, whom he had personally invited down from Ohio. Further,

Bishop Gallagher was accused of mishandling funds, specifically of depriving the Sisters of Charity of the Incarnate Word of $8,000 they wished to use for an orphanage in Galveston. These statements were revealed in a petition written by several laymen. The Apostolic Delegate to the United States, Cardinal Francesco Satolli, was touring the United States at that time. The Cardinal actually received a copy of this petition while in New Orleans. The Cardinal urged Bishop Gallagher not to share the petition but insisted that the Ursuline Convent Chapel remain open.

Bishop Gallagher asked Archbishop Janssens, the Archbishop of New Orleans, to help with the delicate matter. Although the Archbishop would not come to Galveston, as it would draw attention to the matter, he was willing to assist Bishop Gallagher. The Archbishop also urged Bishop Gallagher to reopen the Ursuline Convent to the public, noting that it was a convenient place for individuals to stop by for a few moments of prayer. He further urged him to place a trustworthy priest at the Cathedral who would have his confidence and that of the parishioners. This recommendation from Archbishop Janssens led the Bishop to call upon Fr. James Kirwin to come to the Diocese of Galveston from Circleville, Ohio. Fr. Kirwin was ordained in 1895 and sent to study at Catholic University for a year. He arrived in Galveston in 1896. Over time, he helped alleviate many of the remaining tensions.

[9] Bishop Claude Dubuis
Bishop of Galveston (1862-1892)

[9] Bishop Claude Dubuis—Castroville Area Chamber of Commerce.

[10]Archbishop Francis Janssens
Archbishop of New Orleans (1888-1897)

[10] Archbishop Francis Janssens—St. Louis Cathedral, New Orleans.

Chapter Two

Fr. James Kirwin – or Big Jim

James Kirwin came from Ohio, as Bishop Gallagher had. Undoubtedly, they crossed paths as Kirwin went through his seminary training there in Ohio and remained there the years immediately following. Gallagher must have had some inkling of the giftedness in the young seminary student.

James Martin Kirwin was born in the town of Circleville, Ohio, on July 1, 1872. His parents were seen as pioneers in the industrial sector, working with the Western Railway Company and the North Fork Railway Company. They were of Irish ancestry. His father, Patrick, was seen as honest and industrious. His mother, Mary Ryan, was recognized as carrying out her duties of Christian motherhood in an honorable fashion. They taught their children in the practice of their Catholic faith, including daily prayer. The family would gather every evening around their home altar to recite the rosary. The bookshelves were filled with volumes of solid moral and philosophical principles, in addition to providing a background in history. In this home, the seeds of religion, virtue, and patriotism were sown. It was here also that the children learned to obey the just laws of their country.[1]

---

[1] Stephen P. Brown, Student of the Monsignor, "Monsignor James M. Kirwin," *Memoirs of Monsignor James Kirwin,* George T. Elmendorf, Compiler, n.p.

James Kirwin began his education at the age of six in the public schools, later followed by further training in the Catholic schools. Upon completion of his primary grades, he was sent to St. Joseph's College in Bardstown, Kentucky. He finished his college work at St. Mary's College in Lebanon, Kentucky, receiving a B.A. in 1890. He became a clerical student at St. Mary of the West in Cincinnati, Ohio, and there completed his courses in Theology and Philosophy. During this time, he was further recognized as an advocate of athletic pursuits. He and another seminarian, Michael J. Kelly, wrote a history of the Seminary. We received it as a well-written history of the institution. This seminary was also the alma mater of Bishop Nicholas Gallagher. James Kirwin was ordained to the priesthood at Mt. St. Mary's Seminary of the West Chapel by Archbishop William Henry Elder on June 15, 1895. He was sent off to study Theology at the Catholic University of America by Bishop Gallagher and completed it in 1896. He was incardinated into the diocese of Galveston at the request of Bishop Gallagher.[2]

Upon Fr. Kirwin's arrival in the diocese of Galveston, Bishop Gallagher appointed him as rector of the Cathedral. The new pastor immediately entered the parish's spiritual life. He originated the Young Men's Institute, which promoted a higher standard of Christian living. Catholic Knights of America, Branch 166, made Kirwin their spiritual director. He was likewise the spiritual director of the Young Ladies' Sodality and the Children of Mary.[3]

---

[2] Ibid.

[3] Ibid.

Fr. Kirwin urged the citizens of Galveston to adopt proper sanitation practices during the yellow fever epidemic, which broke out in 1897. He was readily called upon to console the sick and the dying. As a result of his selfless service, his parishioners grew in admiration of him.[4]

[5] Birthplace of Father Kirwin at Circleville, Ohio

[4] Ibid.

[5] Birthplace of Father Kirwin in Circleville, Ohio, *Memoirs of Monsignor James Kirwin,* George T. Elmendorf, Compiler, n.p.

The Kirwin family Group of Circleville, Ohio [6]

James M. Kirwin as a Young Man [7]

---

[6] The Kirwin Family Group of Circleville, Ohio, *The Memoirs of Monsignor James M. Kirwin,* George T. Elmendorf, Compiler, n.p.

[7] James M. Kirwin as a Young Man, *Memoirs of Monsignor James M. Kirwin,* George T. Elmendorf, Compiler, n.p.

One person who was a great inspiration to James Kirwin on his journey to the priesthood was Fr. MM Meara, who hailed from Columbus, Ohio. Kirwin wrote a tribute to Fr. Meara, which was published in booklet form and eventually became part of the Catholic Record Society. In this biographical document, James Kirwin pointed out that Fr. Meara arrived at St. Joseph's Church in Circleville, Ohio, in April 1882. He was known for having a "charming personality." He was "a manly character." Realizing a need for a parochial school, he won the parishioners over. Thus, by 1886, the school was fully paid for and opened for $20,000. The Sisters of Charity of Nazareth took care of the teaching. They were known for their "tender, uplifting care." The building consisted of twelve rooms plus a convent for the Sisters.

Fr. Meara was recognized as a "devoted" pastor, whether he was responding to the call of the sick, correcting the lazy, arousing the indifferent, or conquering the incorrigible. He was further, "the soul of hospitality." Fr. Meara could win over those he came in contact with. He lived for the school and its students. The school soon became recognized as 'the best in the state."

Kirwin actually paid tribute to Fr. Meara in his last Mass, January 24, 1926.[8]

---

[8] Msgr. James Kirwin, "Rev. Michael Mary Meara The Greatest Gift of God-the Priest," *Barquilla dela Santa Maria, Bulletin of the Catholic Record Society, Diocese of Columbus, Vol. XXXV, No. 1, January, 2010, January 24 , Rev. M.M. Meara.*

Fr. Meara and Fr. Kirwin [9]

The Spanish-American War

The United States went to war with Spain in 1898. The city of Galveston chose to form a volunteer unit. Fr. Kirwin gave such a patriotic speech that many men signed up, and they chose him as chaplain. The War Department confirmed that choice and gave him the rank of Captain. When this unit of men was at Camp Hawly, they outfitted Fr. Kirwin with a horse saddle and all that goes with it. He celebrated Mass for the men every Sunday morning and, after

---

[9] "Fr. Meara and Fr. Kirwin," *Memoirs of Monsignor James M. Kirwin*, George T. Elmendorf, Compiler, n.p.

Mass, preached a sermon on the day's Gospel. He urged the men to take their responsibilities seriously in serving their country, for the country depended on them to win the war. There were no benches. The men had to kneel on the ground. He was much respected by the soldiers for his service to them. He received an honorable discharge from the service in October 1898. He thus became a member of the Spanish War Veterans. He attended all of their annual reunions. He was frequently asked to deliver the historical address at the annual meeting. Following his service, he rejoined parish life at the Cathedral.[10]

The Spanish-American War ended Spain's control of colonies in the Western Hemisphere. Fighting among Cuban revolutionaries took place from 1595 to 1598 to end Spanish colonial rule. There was much sympathy in the United States for Cuban revolutionaries. When the Battleship Maine exploded in Havana harbor under "mysterious circumstances, on February 15, 1898, American intervention followed. President McKinley asked Congress to end the war in Cuba and establish a "stable government." Thus, Congress passed a resolution asking Spain to cede control of Cuba and granted McKinley the authority to use whatever military force was necessary to secure Cuban independence. The Spanish government refused the ultimatum and declared war on the United States. The United States declared war on Cuba. The war ended on December 10, 1898, with the signing of the Treaty of Paris. Cuba was guaranteed its independence. Guam and Puerto Rico were ceded to the United States, and

---

[10]Stephen P. Brown, Student of the Monsignor, "Monsignor James M. Kirwin," *Memoirs of Monsignor James M. Kirwin,* George T. Elmendorf, Compiler, n p.

the Philippines was sold to the United States for $20,000,000. The Senate accepted the peace treaty with a margin of one vote. A group of Hawaiian-based planters sought annexation by the United States. A joint resolution of Congress made this a reality on August 12, 1898. [11]

The war ended on December 10, 1898, with the signing of the Treaty of Paris. Cuba was guaranteed its independence. Guam and Puerto Rico were ceded to the United States. A group of Hawaiian-based planters sought annexation by the United States. A joint resolution of Congress made this a reality on August 12, 1898. [12]

[13] Fr. James Martin Kirwin, Chaplain
First US Volunteer Regiment, Spanish-American War

---

[11] "Office of the Historian, Foreign Service Institute, United States Department of State," and Anibal A. Gonzalez, "Kirwin, James Martin," *Handbook of Texas Online. https://tshaonline.org/handbook/entries/kirwin-james-martin. Published by the Texas State Historical Association.*

[12] Ibid.

[13] Fr. James Martin Kirwin, Chaplain, First US Volunteer Regiment, Spanish American War, *Memoirs of Monsignor James M. Kirwin,* George T. Elmendorf, Compiler, n.p.

[14] General John J. Pershing (1860-1948)

"Black Jack"

Mexican Expedition

American Expeditionary Force

Offered to Fr. Kirwin the General Chaplainship

to all American forces under his command

---

[14] Pbs.org.

[15] Fr. James Kirwin with General J.A.Hulen
At San Antonio, Texas, May, 1916

---

[15] Father James Kirwin with General J.A. Hulen at San Antonio, Texas, May 1916, *Memoirs of Monsignor James M. Kirwin,* George T. Elmendorf, Compiler, n.p.

Before, During, and After World War I

The 144th Infantry Regiment is an infantry regiment of the US Army, Texas Army National Guard. It was formed in 1880 and has served in several American wars. The 144th was created in 1880 when six volunteer militia companies of the Texas State Guard consolidated into the Fourth Texas State Infantry. In 1898, the Fourth Texas Volunteers were called forth into federal service in the Spanish-American War. [16]

Fr. Kirwin served as the chaplain of the Fourth Texas Infantry on the border with Mexico in 1915. He became the spiritual guide to many of these men in the State militia. As a result, he was one of the most popular men in the militia.

General John J. Pershing cabled Fr. Kirwin from Cherbourg, France, in 1917. H asked him to come immediately to serve as a Chaplain in France. General McCain issued him a First Lieutenant's Commission. Fr. Kirwin put his affairs in order and set out for France. He got as far as New York when he was told that Bishop Gallagher had passed away. Fr. Kirwin immediately returned to Galveston to attend to matters within the diocese.

During World War I, patriotic civilians supported the war effort by giving four-minute speeches in movie houses, for it took four minutes to change a reel. Commercial radio was still several years away. More than 75,000 civilians participated, and more than four hundred million listeners heard these speeches. This endeavor was

[16] Texas Military Department, Office of the Governor.

part of the Liberty Loan Drives. [17] While he was very involved in the affairs of the Galveston diocese, Fr. Kirwin aided the Liberty Loan Drive by serving as a four-minute speaker. Their goal was to walk away with signed pledges. The Red Cross needed workers, and priests were needed in the army training camps. After the war, Fr. Kirwin was involved in post-war reconstruction.

Above is the coat of arms and unit crest of the 144th Infantry Regiment, Par Oneri, "equal to the task." The shield is blue for the

[17] J. Graham, "Four Minute Men News," Committee on Public Information, Taylor and Francis Online.

infantry. The crest at the top stands for the Texas National Guard. The wavy, diagonally oriented lines bound by borders refer to the Regiment's service along the Mexican border. [18]

[19] World War I Bonds

[18]Texas Military Department, Texans Serving Texas.

[19] World War I Liberty Loan Posters, Library of Congress.

[20]

[21]

World War I Liberty Loan Posters

[22] Group of Teaching Staff and Student Body at St. Mary's Seminary, La Porte, Texas

---

[20] WWI Liberty Loan Poster, Air Force Museum

[21] War Bond Poster, Museum of the American G.I.

[22] "Group of Teaching Staff and Student Body at St. Mary's Seminary, La Porte, Texas," *Memoirs of Monsignor James M. Kirwin,* George T. Elmendorf, Compiler, n. p.

Bishop Gallagher chose Fr. Kirwin to serve as President of St. Mary's Seminary after the Basilians withdrew over a disagreement with the Bishop. Bishop Gallagher also asked him to teach Moral Theology and serve as vicar general. This role required a working knowledge of canon law. Msgr. Kirwin graciously accepted each position. He "buried" himself in the diocesan seminary. He certainly realized that he would not have an outlet for many of his abilities. Those who saw him in "disfavor" and who could be called his "enemies" owe him their promotion. He made every effort to advance a deserving individual, even though it meant that someone dear to him would lose out. Whenever there was a question of his promotion and duty, he let the promotion go and did his priestly duty. [23]

As a schoolmaster, Monsignor taught Latin and Spanish. He was known for tutoring seminarians in the evening who were a bit behind in a particular academic area. As a seminary professor, he lectured in Theology and Philosophy. Monsignor Kirwin was unusually gifted in the power of persuasion. He could lead because he had first learned how to follow. He knew how to give orders because he had already learned to follow. He knew how to give necessary orders because he had learned how to take and obey orders. He was a person one enjoyed meeting. He was generous in his judgment of others. [24]

Before coming to Texas, this gentleman had heard that the vicar general of the diocese was a square man who gave everyone a square

---

[23]Rev. Stephen P. Brown, *Memoirs of Monsignor James M. Kirwin*, George T. Elmendorf, Compiler, n. p.

[24] Edgar Odell Lovett, Ph.D. "Monsignor Kirwin as Educator," *Memoirs of Monsignor James M. Kirwin*, George T. Elmendorf, Compiler, n.p.

deal. On his way to Galveston, a former student, who had been ordained a priest, told this gentleman that he would like Monsignor Kirwin. Everyone does. He teaches Moral Theology. One derives more from a few words from him than from a long talk from someone else. As he was part of a tutoring session with Monsignor to catch up on Theology, Monsignor showed no irritability or impatience. He gave much yet expected little. [25]

---

[25] Rev. Thomas A. Ryan, "A Foot Soldier of Jesus Christ," *Memoirs of Monsignor James M. Kirwin,* George T. Elmendorf, Compiler, n. p.

Chapter Three

The 1900 Storm

The view of the Galveston storm varied by location on the island. At least six thousand people died during that storm. People in Galveston had been hearing of a coming storm, but, unfortunately, the inhabitants did little by way of preparation. When the long-distance wire to Houston snapped at 3:00 pm, Galveston was isolated from the world. Solid buildings began to collapse. The weathermen's instruments blew away at 5:15 pm. The last recorded velocity was 84 mph with gusts at 110 to 120. [1]

Bishop Gallagher, Fr. Kirwin, and several priests at the Cathedral had no idea they were in one of the better or safer spots. Fr. Kirwin described the slate and tile coming off from various roofs as "a hail of bullets." It appeared that one could be as safe indoors as outdoors. The wind became so strong that one might assume that one's house was being driven away. Such was the case when Bishop Gallagher told Fr. Kirwin to "prepare everyone for death." [2]

---

[1] Sr. Loyola Hegarty, CCVI, *Serving with Gladness, The Origin and History of the Congregation of the Sisters of Charity of the Incarnate Word, Houston, Texas* (Houston, Texas: Bruce Publishing in cooperation with the Sisters of Charity of the Incarnate Word. Houston, Texas, 1967), 321-322.

[2] James Talmadge Moore, *Acts of Faith: The Catholic Church in Texas, 1900-1950* (College Station, Texas: Texas A & M University Press, 2002), 24-25.

St. Mary's Infirmary cast a very different picture. Many inhabitants had sought refuge in the sturdier hospital buildings, for the frame buildings had collapsed. Almost every window was broken. Part of the roof had blown away. Monsignor John Gleissner, from St. Joseph Parish in Bryan, was there recuperating from surgery. By mid-afternoon, water was already at the hospital gate. Water from the Gulf had already met Galveston Bay. Inhabitants from the hospital moved from the first to the second floor when they could no longer stay on the first. The staff that remained took care of the seriously injured. Many of the refugees coming in were hysterical as they had seen members of their family swept away to death. The lights went out, leaving the inhabitants in the dark. They struggled to keep the chapel vigil light. Fr. Gleissner carried the Eucharist around the hospital every hour to offer comfort to all. Soon, the waters began to recede, a sign of great hope. However, when light came, the power of devastation set in. The first supply of drinking water and bread came from Beaumont and Houston. Individuals came to St. Mary's Infirmary looking for their loved ones. What joy there was when they found them, what sadness when the search was in vain. [3]

Ursuline Convent served as a shelter for 1,500 people that night, despite the storm severely damaging the building. They kept pulling in people who were floating by on wreckage. In an age of segregation, blacks and whites were next to each other and did not seem to mind. The bells rang continually through the night to direct people to the convent, that place of shelter. The Dominican convent became a hospital for storm survivors. They already had 30 students for the

---

[3] Ibid., 322, 326.

fall semester, in addition to 50 Sisters. Sacred Heart Church did not survive, and the University buildings were severely damaged. Half of the parishioners of Sacred Heart parish did not survive. [4]

[5] St. Mary's Infirmary before the 1900 Storm

[4] Sr. Sheila Hackett, O.P., *Dominican Women in Texas, From Ohio to Galveston and Beyond* (Houston, TX: Sacred Heart Convent, 1986), 109, Moore, *Acts of Faith, 25.*

[5] St. Mary's Infirmary before the 1900 Storm, Courtesy of Rosenberg Library.

[6] St. Mary's Infirmary after the Storm

[6] St. Mary's Infirmary after the Storm, courtesy of Rosenberg Library.

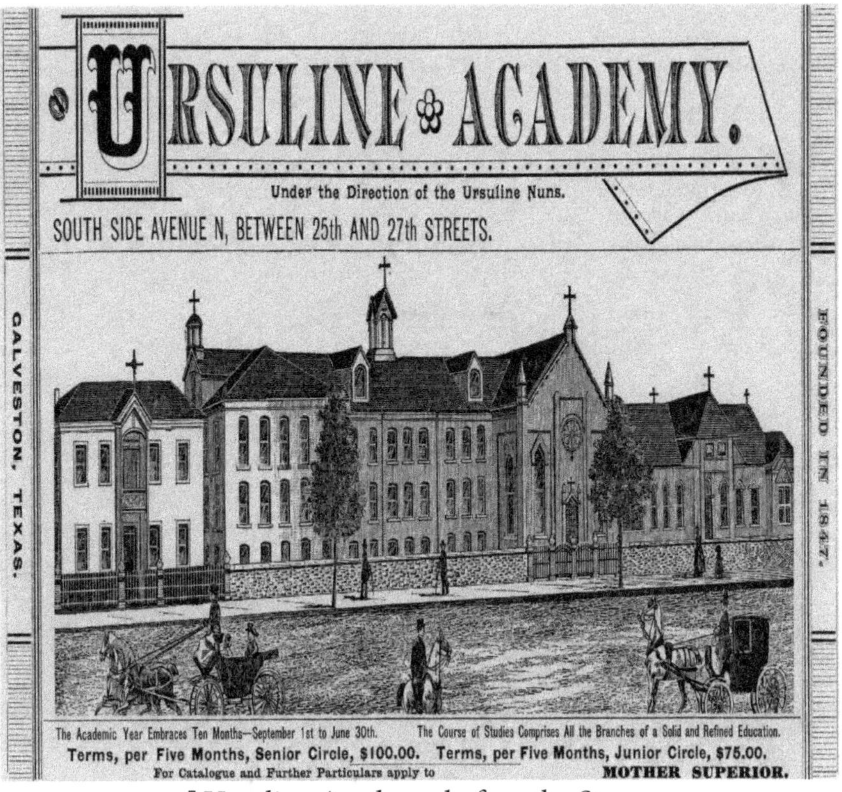

[7] Ursuline Academy before the Storm

---

[7] Ursuline Academy before the Storm, courtesy Rosenberg Library.

[8] Ursuline Academy after the Storm

What the Sisters found at the orphanage site was not expected. Ninety-four orphans and ten Sisters perished in the storm. There was no sign that the orphanage had ever been there. Some of the Sisters had tied themselves to smaller children in a futile attempt to save them. The three boys who managed to survive stated they were in the chapel, praying. Then the building collapsed. They found themselves clinging to a tree. Then they realized they were on a pile of debris near the post office. Every year, the Sisters of Charity of the

[8] Ibid.

Incarnate Word sing "Queen of the Waves" in honor of the ten Sisters who gave their lives for these little children. [9]

Mrs. Laura Green chose the orphanage's location. A fervent Catholic, yet in a childless marriage, she had specified that the proceeds from the sale of her home would benefit the construction of St. Patrick's Church and the parish's orphans. She herself was a great lover of children. This allowed for the expansion of facilities for the orphans. It was in 1873 that Bishop Dubuis was looking for a new home for the orphans, and therefore, the location on property originally owned by Mrs. Laura Green came about. [10]

[11] Sisters of Charity Orphanage, about 1890

[9] Hegarty, 324-330.

[10] Hegarty, 230-232.

[11] 1900 Storm Galveston, Texas.

On Sept. 8, 1994, a Texas Historical Marker was placed at 69th Street and Seawall Boulevard, marking the site of the former orphanage. [12] The descendants of two of the survivors, Will Murny and Frank Madera, returned to participate in the marker dedication. As part of the ceremony, "Queen of the Waves" was again sung at the same time and place as it was during the Great 1900 Storm. And, as it continues to be each Sept. 8 by the Sisters of Charity of the Incarnate Word.

---

[12] 1900 Storm Galveston, Texas. On Sept. 8, 1994, a Texas Historical Marker was placed at 69th Street and Seawall Boulevard, marking the site of the former orphanage. *Linda Macdonald is Director of Communications, Congregation of the Sisters of Charity of the Incarnate Word in Houston.*

In March of 1901, a new orphanage was opened on 40th and Q streets. The new brick home would accommodate 90 children. A few years later, in 1912, Dr. and Mrs. F. K. Fisher gave a block of ground adjacent to the orphanage for a playground in memory of their nephew J. Kenner Fisher. The orphanage later received aid from the Community Chest and Catholic Charities. [13]

Clara Barton, the founder of the Red Cross, arrived to assist efforts after the storm. The Red Cross was only nineteen years old at that time. The agency members, coming down from Washington, D.C., established an orphanage for storm victims and helped to acquire lumber to rebuild homes. The organization raised money by selling photos of the disaster. The Red Cross and the New York World newspaper shared Headquarters at 25th and Strand Streets

[13] Hegarty, 397.

after the storm. Clara Barton, in her written report of the disaster, said that her workers had grown "pale and ill." She herself needed a steady hand to help get her back to the Pullman on the track, waiting free of charge. It was her last disaster effort, as she was 78. [14]

North of Galveston, in the Houston area, St. Joseph Church was severely damaged, as was First Baptist, Shearn Memorial Methodist, and Christ Episcopal Church. In fact, as far north as Industry, Sealy, and Brenham, Catholic churches were severely damaged. None of this compares to the damage in Galveston, however. [15]

Within the devastated city, Fr. Kirwin and several other citizens, fifteen in all, met on the street corner in several feet of water to form the Committee on Public Safety. They met at the Tremont Hotel. Fr. Kirwan wrote the order to place the city under martial law to prevent looting and violence. He was also very much involved in the formation of a Central Relief Committee to provide food and clothing for those in need. This Committee fed between 17,000 and 20,000 a day. They worked through the wards in the city. A very difficult challenge was met with the disposal of the dead bodies. At first, the members of the committee believed the bodies could be buried at sea. That failed when the decomposed bodies washed back to shore. The only other alternative was burning the bodies with lumber from the destroyed buildings. This was done with the greatest reverence possible. A census bureau was established to count the living and the

---

[14] Don Peak, and Clara Barton, "A Story of the Red Cross," plus information drawn from the Galveston County Historical Museum and the Rosenberg Library, Galveston.

[15] Moore, *Acts of Faith*, 25.

dead.[16] Eventually, telephone and rail transportation were provided. Shops began to open up. Galveston began to experience that it was on the road to rehabilitation.[17]

One of the first acts of the Central Relief Committee following the storm was to send a letter of gratitude to Clara Barton and the American Red Cross. Mayor Jones, Chairman of the Committee, formulated with members of the Committee the following resolutions, which were unanimously adopted:

> Whereas, the people of Galveston have been the beneficiaries of the noble charity and experienced relief of the American National Red Cross, and the Central Relief Committee has had the invaluable counsel of Miss Clara Barton, President, and Mr. Stephen E. Barton, Vice-President, therefore be it
>
> *Resolved,* That for ourselves we acknowledge the assistance and the inspiration of Miss Barton and Mr. Barton in the perplexing duties to which we were called; that we regret their departure but realize that it is the economy of their mission to the world they cannot remain with us longer.
>
> *Resolved,* That for our people we have found relief under the sheltering arm of the Red Cross and consolation in the overwhelming love of its consecrated agents; we hereby express the everlasting gratitude of a community which has

---

[16] Stephen P. Brown, Student of the Monsignor, "Monsignor James M. Kirwin," *Memoirs of Monsignor James Kirwin,* George T. Elmendorf, Compiler, n.p.

[17] Ibid.

been lifted out of its sorrows into the dawn of new hopes and out of its losses into the resolution of a new life.

Resolved, That we recommend to the world the great organization whose efficiency and tenderness have been demonstrated to us during the last two months, and we appeal to civilization for the maintenance of this surpassing institution, which knows no country but the desolate places and no class or race but stricken humanity wherever it is found upon the globe.

Resolved, That we especially thank and render homage to the woman who is the life and spirit of the Red Cross. She who is the embodiment of the saving principle of laying down one's life for one's friend, whose friend is the friendless and whose charge is the stricken, and who should be exalted above Queens and whose achievements are greater than the conquests of nations or the inventions of genius, and who is justly crowned in the evening of her life with the love and admiration of all humanity,

MISS CLARA BARTON

Mr. Jens Moller, of the Committee, in speaking to the above resolutions, among other things said: "It proves to us more strongly than ever, after the experience we have had since the arrival of Miss Barton, that 'Woman rules the world,' as she has always done. Miss Barton, in her noble calling, rules for the better. There is not, and there could not be, a nobler work in the world than that in which Miss Barton and her Society are engaged, and may God grant that we and her children and our children's children will ever hold in fond recollection the sacrifices of Miss Barton and her assistants and their noble acts of charity in Galveston during the dark days following the storm of the 8th of September, 1900.

Reply of Miss Clara Barton to the Central Relief Committee of Galveston, Washington, D.C., April 19, 1901,

> To the Members of the Central Relief Committee of Galveston.
>
> Gentlemen and Friends:-
>
> When we contrast this day and this occasion with those which first brought us together, what words can express that contrast? What sensations can possess the mind but wonder and adoration for the power of Almighty God and a humble gratitude that no words can speak.
>
> In one night, plunged into the depths of woe, desolation, horror, and dismay, never equaled by any community in our land. Less than seven months ago, with this consternation overhanging you, its attendant horrors creeping through your veins, with a charge of ten thousand dead and thirty thousand living upon your hearts and hands, we met as strangers. Your mighty task is performed—the dead rest. The living are again in the ways of ordinary life, and your beautiful city once more showing signs of its former thrift, activity, prosperity, and loveliness; its institutions of charity, industry, and learning are rising again, phoenix-like, from

the ashes of the past,-new homes bedeck the streets, the perfume of flowers and the merry laugh of childhood enliven its borders.

A herculean task indeed, but what body of people ever performed so great a task so well?

Justice of administration has set its seal forever on your integrity of purpose, unanimity has marked the greatness of soul above all narrow selfishness, and forbearance has revealed the Divine Spirit of the Master, which must have animated every heart and ruled every act.

And now in only this short space of time, this earnest perplexed committee of men has found the moment and had the grace of thought to meet and to express thanks to those who went to them strangers, with no feeling but pity, no thought, but to carry to them the spirit of the symbol they wore, and, in its name, to offer such aid as might be rendered humbly.

Gentlemen, the magnificent return you make leaves us breathless—a tribute of honor, of which our English tongue does not surpass.

We accept this tribute with pride and with humility, with frankness and veneration. It shall hold the place of honor in the home it comes to adorn, and the prayers of earnest hearts shall rise for the resurrection of the stricken city and the ever-welfare of those who have been its saviors.

We have the honor to be with highest respect,

Yours,

Clara Barton,

President, American National Red Cross

Stephen E. Barton,

Second Vice-President,

American National Red Cross

[18] Clara Barton (1821-1912)

Foundress of the American Red Cross

---

[18]Women's history.org.

Chapter Four

The Home Protective League

The Texas Constitution, approved in 1876, allowed counties in the state to have their citizens decide whether they wished to be wet or dry. Over time, Texas became increasingly dry. The Temperance movement was very active in the United States in the nineteenth century. Texas was no exception.

However, the Home Protective League sought neither wet nor dry. Rather, the advocates sought a middle ground between prohibition and what was termed "unbridled license." Specifically, there was a strong desire to remove alcohol sales from corner grocery stores or residential areas. They were not going after downtown saloons or beach resorts. They believed this to be a reasonable regulation of alcohol in the city of Galveston. As the members of the Home Protective League pointed out, the neighborhood bar room would be an enemy of the downtown saloon. Unfortunately, this districting ordinance was declared void by the state Supreme Court due to a technical error. The Home Protective League in no way saw this prospective measure as approaching prohibition.

At the time this measure was proposed, January 29, 1909, Fr. James Kirwin served as Vice-President of the Home Protective League. It is interesting to note that Rabbi Cohen, a longtime friend of Bishop Gallagher, was also active in this group.

In an editorial opinion from the *Galveston Tribune*, reprinted by the Home Protective League, a delaying tactic was to call forth an amendment requiring an election before the measure could take effect—naturally, those who do not desire the measure hope for defeat. At best, they look toward delay. The *Galveston Tribune*, in its editorial opinion, reminded its readers that the Texas Brewers' Association is bound to correct the error made in the original amendment. That charter amendment had received the approval of the brewing industry and those in the Texas legislature. The ordinance had been adopted by the board of city commissioners, who were representatives of the citizens of Galveston, after "two patient hearings at which the residence section saloon keepers were represented by eminent counsel." The editorial writers went on to say that if the district charter amendment had to be submitted for a vote, it would create much confusion and prove "highly objectionable in many ways." That was not done in Dallas, Fort Worth, or Beaumont. Those promoting the ordinance were certainly not prohibitionists. As the authors of the editorial continued, "Galveston is susceptible of being made a beautiful residence city, but this fond hope will never be realized until the corner barrooms are removed from the residence section." It brought forth such terminology as fearless and persevering in promoting the ordinance.

The Home Protective League was very clear in stating that it was not a temperance organization. They were not promoting candidates. They were not urging people to pay their poll tax. The liquor business requires strict supervision and an "adequate and faithful police force." The force needed to be placed within "well-defined and reasonable limits." Homes should be found in places of restful quiet. The cheap dive was seen as the greatest of schools of crime. "Are you willing to have a barroom next door to your home? What does your wife think about it? The grocery department became an excuse for cooks and female servants to patronize the bar. Unthinking parents often sent defenseless boys and girls to carry home buckets and pitchers of beer." Of course, minors are not supposed to be buying alcohol. "A man's home is his kingdom. It is for his home, his wife and children, and for their welfare that he works and strives."

The Home Protective League of Galveston included a copy of a revised Saloon Districting Bill that the Legislature was asked to pass for Galveston. It was seen as more liberal than the previous effort, the Home Protective Bill. As stated in its publication, it supported two hundred saloons. [1]

Fortunately, largely due to the efforts of Fr. James Kirwin, the Home Protective League was successful in removing saloons from residential areas in Galveston. The League further lobbied the state legislature for a law that would enable cities to restrict saloons.

Eventually, the Anti-Saloon League groups addressed large crowds in Galveston. This came in the form of revivals and other gatherings. This promoted dry counties in the Galveston area and other arenas in Texas, making it easier for a prohibition majority to take hold. [2]

---

[1] "The Home Protective League," Galveston, TX, v. 1, No. 3, January 29, 1909.

[2] "Anti-Saloon League Workers Address Large Crowds Here." *The Galveston Daily News, Monday, March 31, 1918,* and "Speed Final Decision on Dry Measures," *San Antonio Light,* Saturday, March 16, 1918.

[3] Home Protective League, January 29, 1909 Publication

---

[3]Home Protective League, January 29, 1909, Courtesy of Rosenberg Library.

Chapter Five

The Ku Klux Klan

The origins of the Klan have not been as clear in history as one might assume. The Honorable Thomas W. Gregory of Austin, Texas, one of the foremost lawyers in the nation, was addressing the Arkansas and Texas Bar Associations on July 10, 1906. He addressed the group's origins, noting that it originally sought to curb the excesses of Andrew Johnson's administration. Specifically, Gregory referred to the federal government's sweeping aside of legal and constitutional rights. He pointed out that the KKK was actually in order. Amazingly, the speaker stated that if it were between 1866 and 1872, every man in the audience would have belonged to the KKK or sympathized. Naturally, he did not approve of the crime connected with the movement. It had been a time when thousands of Negroes left the farm and moved into the towns. Unfortunately, agents of the Freedmen's Bureau and local judges were largely prejudiced against native whites. The establishment of the Freedmen's Bureau had traveled a rather rocky road through Congress. [1] In some cases, these judges were profoundly ignorant, as evidenced by their inability to write a return on a writ.

The speaker provided a lengthy list of excesses by the federal government. Some of these thousands of Negroes who moved into the towns were armed and organized into militias. White women experienced ill treatment due to the insolent attitude and drunken

[1] "Freedmen's Bureau Acts of 1865 and 1866," United States Senate.

spirit of some Negroes. Men and women were "frequently" arrested without charge, taken forty or fifty miles away, and imprisoned for an indefinite period without ever appearing before a judge. One such example was that influential white men were disenfranchised, that is, not allowed to vote, as soldiers stood by the ballot box.[2] All of this existed in addition to the dishonesty of the carpetbaggers and scalawags in the post-Civil War South.

The masked riders who appeared intended to create fear among the newly freed Negroes. However, practice sometimes extended much further in the sense of whipping and even hanging the newly freed Negro. Due to the secret character of the KKK, they were unable to defend themselves against false accusations. By 1873, Congress passed legislation assuring the right to vote to all men. This, in turn, quelled the extremes of the KKK movement. Was the rise of the KKK movement justified immediately following the Civil War? Within the view of the Honorable Thomas W. Gregory, it was. He was considering the policies of then-President Andrew Johnson and the perils of Reconstruction.[3]

The Ku Klux Klan in the 1920's

The KKK in the 1920's did not have the excesses of the carpetbaggers or the scalawags, but it did follow the excesses of the KKK, which existed earlier.

---

[2] "Original K.K.K. Worked for Order," *The Galveston Daily News*, Sunday, July 3, 1921.

[3] Ibid.

The Klan of the 1920's actually began with William Joseph Simmons in Atlanta, Georgia, in 1915. However, the movement moved to Dallas, becoming known as Klan no. 66. It picked up the excesses of the KKK after the Civil War, using violence and various forms of intimidation to attempt to curtail the rights of African Americans. The movement also possessed its own strains of anti-Catholicism, anti-Judaism, and nativism. The group, however, engaged in charitable activities, taking on the appearance of a fraternal group. It had a tremendous effect on the Democratic party, especially in Texas. [4]

Unfortunately, historians generally agree that the Klan was more violent in Texas in the 1920s than in any other state. It made its public debut by parading down a dark Main Street of Dallas in May of 1921. The Klan became known when an African American bellhop was abducted at the Adolphus Hotel in Dallas by Hiram Evans and a group of Klansmen. He was taken to a remote location and branded KKK on his forehead. The guilty party suffered no consequences. Other beatings of African Americans followed in the spring of 1922. A Jewish picture frame maker was beaten, and a Dallas police officer was brought to trial but acquitted. The District Attorney, Maury Harris, originally a Klan member who quit over the violence, attempted to go after Klan members but could not move the police force. Louis Turley, the police commissioner, was also a Klan member; the involvement of the police in the Klan put pressure on any action to take place. Several politicians took on the fight against the Klan, including the former Texas governor Oscar Colquitt and

---

[4] Amber Jolly and Ted Banks, "Dallas Klan No. 66," *Handbook of Texas Online*, https://www.tshaonline.org/handbook/entries/dallas-ku-klux-klan-no-66.

former Texas Attorney General Martin Crane. The Dallas County Citizens' League wished to purge from public office any Klan members. [5]

Eventually, three newspapers, the *Dallas Morning News, The Dallas Journal,* and *The Dallas Dispatch,* took on public opposition to the Klan. The *Dallas Morning News* published anti-Klan editorials after such an expose.

Some businessmen took on what appeared to be friendly practices to the Klan. The owner of Schepps Bakery paid for Klan membership for fifty employees, as he said, to monitor their activities. One Jewish-owned business bought advertising in the Klan newspaper, *100 Per Cent American.* Undoubtedly, he did not wish to have his business boycotted. The Dallas Klan did attempt to cultivate an image of philanthropy and civil leadership. This included several carnivals, dances, and barbeques. The most well-known was the Klan Day at the State Fair of Texas held on October 24, 1923. Over 150,000 people were in attendance. By the end of 1923, the Klan dominated the political scene in Dallas. A Klan candidate, Felix Robertson, ran against the infamous Ma Ferguson for governor but lost in a run-off. [6]

Due to the mishandling of funds within Klan No. 66 in Dallas, there was conflict within the membership. This led to a decline in membership. By the end of 1928, membership had declined significantly. A smaller group of Klansmen in Dallas did kidnap and flog two members of the Communist Party in 1931. The Klan's

---

[5] Ibid.

[6] Ibid.

prominence in Dallas had passed, however. The Klan's hub in Texas was moved to San Antonio. One may ask why the Klan had gained such prominence in Dallas. It needs to be brought to one's awareness the philanthropic aspect of the KKK. They distributed food baskets to the poor and cash donations to people in need. A major project was Hope Cottage, an orphanage run by the Klan under the name Klanhaven. It was dedicated at the State Fair Klan Day. The KKK managed that program until it no longer had the funds to do so.[7]

As a result of the Klan's entering into politics in Texas, candidates for office realized that religious liberty was at stake. The KKK wished to abolish the civil rights of Jewish and Catholic citizens. Therefore, all citizens running for office necessarily had to make a statement on religious liberty. Most candidates believed it essential to include a public statement on the Klan in their platforms. Religious liberty was too valuable a freedom to forfeit.[8]

The Klan also inaugurated a plan to wipe out private and public schools in Texas. When the Texas legislature met in January, Representative A.D. Baker of the 65th district introduced a bill which, if successful, would require every child to attend public schools in the state through the eighth grade. The Klan made it very clear in their publication, *Mayfield's Weekly*, that there were "enough 100 percent Americans in the Texas legislature to make the measure a law." Within their publication, they declared that after the parochial

---

[7] Ibid.

[8] "Religious Liberty at Stake," *The Southern Messenger*, August 10, 1922.

schools had been abolished, they would "drive the Homes of the Good Shepherd from the State."[9]

Oliver Allstrom, an individual from Houston responsible for spreading the teachings of the Klan and increasing its membership, wrote a pamphlet against Monsignor James Kirwin entitled "The Priest and the Flag." He was also responsible for anti-Catholic lecturing. However, after a car accident in Luling, Texas, and recuperating in a Baptist Hospital, he saw the light, as he stated, and announced he was through with the Klan. Asked if he was afraid of Klan persecution, he answered in the negative. Rather, he stated that if he was afraid at all, it was of the good men who had never joined. "I was afraid of their smiles and their pity." Allstrom said that 12,000 enlisted in this "hooded brigade of a maniac's dream." He believed only 3,000 remained in good standing when he spoke. [10]

In other parts of the country during the 1920's, there were numerous incidents involving the Klan. In January of 1923, in Philadelphia, Pennsylvania, the Masonic Grand Lodge of Pennsylvania forbade the Klan from using Masonic property. [11] The mayor of New York City, in December of 1922, Mayor John Francis Hylan, commended the governor of Louisiana, Governor John M. Parker, for branding the Klan as the "outstanding menace to our Republic." On

---

[9] "Texas Ku Klux Klan Aims to Abolish Private and Parochial Schools and Convents of the Good Shepherd," *Southern Messenger*, January 4, 1923.

[10] "Ku Klux Klan Scathingly Denounced by Oliver Allstorm, Former Klan Lecturer Asserts Hooded Organization Rapidly Disintegrating in Texas," *Southern Messenger*, November 1, 1923.

[11] "Masons Outlaw Klan in Pennsylvania. Opposed to Organization Forbid Use of Masonic Property," *Southern Messenger*, January 4, 1923.

another note, the Klan in December of 1922 in Baltimore obtained a tax exemption under the name American Union Inc for the use of its property. When the Tax Court discovered that it was the KKK that owned the property, the KKK was told they would have to file again in the Appeals Tax Court under its rightful name, the Ku Klux Klan.

[12] Flyer for Ku Klux Klan at Dallas State Fair, October 24, 1923

The KKK Beyond Texas

While the Klan was dominant in the political scene in Dallas, Texas, the mayor of Philadelphia was sending detectives to

[12]A flyer for Ku Klux Klan Day at the State Fair of Texas.

investigate the membership campaign that the KKK was carrying on in Pennsylvania, New Jersey, and Delaware. The Klan was seen as "taking the law into its own hands." In Chicago, the Klan was viewed as operating in opposition to public policy. The Klan's membership, further, did not account for its funding from membership dues. It was presumed that a Congressional inquiry would follow into the "invisible empire." [13]

Two years later, the lower house of the state of Illinois passed a bill by overwhelming vote stating it would be unlawful for a person to appear in public while hooded or masked, to conceal his identity for purposes of kidnapping or assaulting with a deadly weapon. A fine and imprisonment could follow a finding of guilt under the proposed law. [14]

Within the state of Indiana, the Klan sponsored anti-Catholic legislation. One was Bible reading in the schools. An anti-parochial school bill was aimed at "sectarian schools." A teachers' garb bill aimed at religious teaching in schools. There was also a bill that would have prohibited adults from approving a document signing away the religious rights of an unborn child. This piece of legislation had to do with non-Catholics in a mixed marriage raising their children Catholic. The pieces of legislation were doomed to failure. [15]

---

[13] "Klan to be Investigated: Federal and Municipal Authorities to Look into the Masked Organization," *Southern Messenger*, October 6, 1921.

[14] "Anti-Klan Bill Passed by Lower Illinois House," *Southern Messenger*, Ma 3, 1923.

[15] "Klan Anti-Catholic Bills in Indiana Are Doomed to Defeat," *Southern Messenger*. January 20, 27.

Further, twenty complaints came from Catholics to Washington, D.C., stating they had lost their positions or been discriminated against in applying because of their religion. These complaints were finally registered with the National Catholic Welfare Conference. Many of those complaining blamed the Klan. The experience of "No Catholic Need Apply" was given. One trustee stated there would be no Catholic teacher in the school if he were elected. [16] However, Klan candidates for mayor and city attorney in Baton Rouge were defeated in the primary election. The heaviest vote ever polled in the history of the city of Baton Rouge was cast. [17]

Sadly, the KKK was involved in more than prospective legislation.

The Klan adopted what was seen as a new tactic toward the Catholic Church. In an attempt to disarm individuals, the circular distributed from Klan headquarters in Atlanta entitled "The Attitude of the Klan Toward the Catholic," declared that the Roman Catholic had the right to worship God as anyone else. It moved on to state that the persecution from the Church is due to the "alleged political activities of the hierarchy." So, if the Roman Catholic Church wishes the Klan to stop its own persecution of the Church, it simply needs to "desert the clergy." Naturally, if there are no clergy, there is no Church. They view the Pope as God's divinely appointed agent "over all governments and peoples on earth." Unfortunately, the KKK

---

[16] "Klan Ousts Many Catholics from School Positions," *The Southern Messenger*, July 24, 1924.

[17] "Klan's Candidates in Baton Rouge Lose Nominations," *The Southern Messenger*, August 3, 1922.

would not recognize the difference between spiritual and political allegiance. [18]

An edition of *The Morning News* on September 9, 1921, reports that the Emperor of the Klan stated that 48,000 members were added to their roster in four months. The Klan listed 214 employees working on commission in a nationwide field. There were eight sales districts or domains. Each of these salesmen was placed under a "special pledge of personal fealty to their 'Emperor.'" This was house-to-house membership peddling at $10.00 per membership donation. [19]

A Methodist minister denounced the burning of crosses from the pulpit. In Flint, Michigan, this minister was found on a street corner in such a pitiable state that he was taken to a hospital. The letters KKK had been branded on his back, two inches tall. Sadly, he could not recall exactly what happened to him. [20]

Unfortunately, Klansmen were responsible for a riot in a small mining town by the name of Lilly in Pennsylvania. The incident took place on April 8, 1924. The townspeople were opposed to any demonstration. The United Mine Workers and the union were opposed to the Klan. Certain members of the Klan had been discharged from their jobs in the mine. People in the town then asked for police protection against the Klan. When the Klansmen boarded their special train at the train station, the crowd tried to turn a fire hose on

---

[18] "Ku Klux Klan Adopts New Tactics," *The Southern Messenger,* August 14, 1924.

[19] "Membership Peddlers Take Special Pledge to Defend Klan Emperor," *The Galveston Daily News,*" September 9, 1921.

[20] "Methodist Minister Branded with "KKK" After Pulpit Sermon," *The Southern Messenger,*" July 24, 1924.

them. The Klansmen fired into the crowd. They stated later that they were defending themselves. Two people were dead, and two were dying, and twenty were seriously wounded. Twenty-four Klansmen were arrested in Johnstown, Pennsylvania, charged with murder and inciting a riot. Klansmen had come to the town on two previous occasions and tried to light fiery crosses, but were driven away.[21]

In the city of Atlanta, the Commissioner of the Board of Education introduced a resolution to dismiss all Catholics from their service. The mayor objected, stating that it was too sweeping. The three Atlanta newspapers denounced the proposal to have Catholic teachers dropped from the public school system. "Atlanta does not deserve this sort of thing," read the headline of an editorial in *The Georgian.* The editorial stated, "Fundamentally, the proposal of the commissioner is unsound and untenable -in violent opposition, indeed, to our most cherished ideals of thought."[22]

Catholic Institutions and the Klan

The Dominican Sisters had established themselves in Galveston at the bidding of Bishop Nicholas Gallagher, who became bishop of Galveston. Sacred Heart Academy served the Sisters and students well. After, however, the infamous storm of 1900, the Sisters were fearful that parents would be hesitant to send their daughters to a boarding school in Galveston. They therefore made arrangements to

[21] "Twenty-Four Klansmen Face Charges of Murder after Lilly Riot," *The Southern Messenger*, April 17, 1924.

[22]"Bigotry in Atlanta, Press Denounces Educational Commissioner's Intolerance," *The Southern Messenger*, May 4, 1922.

purchase the former Methodist college in Lampasas, Texas. It would become the site of St. Dominic's Villa. By 1901, it had electric lights and, a few years later, running water. Sixty boarders came by 1903. Four years later, boarders were coming from across the country.[23] They had made a fast start at a new site. Unfortunately, after World War I, the Ku Klux Klan spread a wave of prejudice against Catholics. St. Dominic's Villa closed in 1925.[24]

St. Vincent Hospital in Sherman, Texas, also had its experiences with the Klan. Founded by the Sisters of Charity of St. Vincent de Paul, the hospital opened in 1903. They were assisted in these early years by the Sisters of St. Mary of Namur, who oversaw St. Joseph Academy. The hospital grew steadily. A school of nursing opened in 1913 and operated until 1931. Several nurses graduating from the hospital nursing school served in World War I. The Sisters were known for their care for the sick and poor. They visited the city prison, brought Christmas baskets to the indigent, and gave medicines to the poor. However, they had several experiences with the Klan. On one occasion, the KKK surrounded the hospital in silence. They made no statement as to what they were objecting to, so they left in silence.[25]

On a much more serious and brutal level, a Catholic priest was severely beaten, tarred, and feathered in the small town of Slaton,

---

[23] James Talmadge Moore, *Acts of Faith, The Catholic Church in Texas, 1900-1950,* (College Station, TX: TX A & M University Press, 2002), 28.

[24] Carlos E. Castañeda, *The Church in Texas since Independence*, v. 7of *Our Catholic Heritage in Texas, 1519-1936 (Austin, TX: Von Boeckmann-Jones, 1958), 337.*

[25] Ibid., 401.

Texas, on March 4, 1922. This was "the result of pro-German accusations made against Fr. J.M. Keller during the World War." The priest himself was accused of being pro-German. A $2,500.00 reward was put out for his assailants. [26] Two priests stationed at St. Patrick's Church in Houston found themselves targets of the Klan. Fr. Bernard Lee was jailed for charges of drunkenness. Parishioners had to post his bail. There was no case against the pastor, however, so the case never went to trial. Fr. John O'Reilly was a native of Ireland. He had criticized President Wilson from the pulpit at St. Patrick's for not promoting Irish Independence at the Versailles Treaty. He was called on phony sick calls. The first time, he was thrown from a moving car into Hermann Park. He had to be hospitalized. The second time, he was tarred and feathered. [27]

The Klan had a demonstration/parade in Wallis, Texas, which has approximately 700 inhabitants. The members of the Klan "ordered" every person who did not support the public schools to leave the town. The film "American Catholics in War and Reconstruction" was stolen from the theater from which it was to be shown. The films were found at the bottom of the Brazos River, about three miles from Wallis. No arrests had been made as of June 30, 2021. [28]

Back again in Texas, an Associated Press dispatch from March 21, 1922, stated that notices had been placed on the doors of the Church of the Blessed Sacrament threatening to dynamite the

---

[26] "Brutal Outrage on a Catholic Priest," *The Southern Messenger*, March 16, 1922.

[27] Moore, 70.

[28] "Ku Klux Outbreak at Wallis, Texas," *Southern Messenger,* July 7, 2021.

Church and tar and feather the pastor. The pastor belonged to the Josephite Order, which specifically serves African Americans. This is a Church operated for an African American populace. A school run by the Sisters of the Blessed Sacrament operates within the Parish. This religious community operates schools, academies, and orphanages for Africans Americans and Indians in various dioceses in the United States. [29] The Knights of Columbus followed with a meeting attended by 1600 to curb such violence and violent threats. Over time, this did happen. [30]

American Catholics needed to compile accurate statistics regarding their participation in the War. This was essential, especially when bigoted groups like the Ku Klux Klan attempted to attack Catholic participation in the War. Otherwise, Daniel Ryan, director of the Department of Historical Records of the National Catholic War Council, stated that the Catholic Church can lay itself open to attack. Seven dioceses had already completed reports showing that they had furnished their quota or more than their quota of men to the War. [31]

Murder in Birmingham

Perhaps the most infamous case illustrating the viciousness and cunning of the Klan took place in Birmingham, Alabama, when a

---

[29] "Threat to Destroy a Catholic Church in Beaumont, Texas," *The Southern Messenger*, March 23, 1922.

[30] Moore, 71.

[31] "Catholic War Records Essential to Refute False Statements of the Ku Klux Klan." *Southern Messenger*, November 2, 1922.

Methodist minister killed an Irish priest, Fr. James Coyle. James Coyle had been trained at the North American College and ordained a priest in Rome in 1896.

When Fr. Coyle sailed for North America, he was stationed in Mobile, Alabama, serving under Bishop Edward Patrick Allen. He became an instructor and then rector of the McGill School for Boys. He was later transferred to Birmingham, Alabama, where he became the pastor of St. Paul's Church, later Cathedral. There, he was well received by the Congregation. He was also a chaplain of the Knights of Columbus.

Catholic and Protestant populations in Birmingham had grown due to the expansion of industry in the area. Unfortunately, some states, such as Alabama, had "convent inspection laws" which allowed police to search convents without search warrants, looking for weapons or kidnapped Protestant women. Fr. Coyle stood up for his parishioners in such an environment. Sadly, he was a target for anonymous death threats.

Edwin Stephenson was actually a Methodist deacon but presented himself to the public as a "full-fledged minister." He was well known in the city of Birmingham because he would spend time in the courthouse, going up and down the hall, offering to officiate at weddings for those in need of a preacher. The courthouse was right next door to St. Paul's Church.

Stephenson's daughter Ruth had been raised there in Birmingham within the Methodist religion. However, as a teenager, she became interested in the Catholic faith and made an appointment with Fr. Coyle to pursue that interest. Before long, at the age of 18, she was baptized into the faith. When her father heard this, he threatened to kill his daughter. Ruth then went to stay with a Catholic family until matters cooled down. Her father told police a Catholic family had kidnapped her. Ruth was returned to her father, who beat her with a razor strap.

Ruth had met a wallpaper hanger, Pedro Gussman, who was twenty-four years older than herself. He had wallpapered the Stephenson house and boarded with them during that time. Gussman had also patronized Stephenson's barber shop. Pedro Gussman did not look his age. She had remained in touch with him over the next several years. Eventually, Gussman proposed to Ruth. Each of them worked in downtown Birmingham. When she accepted the proposal, they planned to marry during their lunch hour. Thus, she and Pedro asked Fr. Coyle to officiate at their wedding. Fr. Coyle had his sister and another priest as witnesses. Since she was 21, she could approach Fr. Coyle to ask for permission to marry this young man. Fr. Coyle realized that she was of legal age. Therefore, her parents' permission was not necessary.

The state of Alabama had a law that prohibited interracial marriage. Edwin Stephenson thought his daughter was dating a black man. Fr. Coyle sat on his front porch every afternoon to pray his Breviary. In that sense, he was available to his parishioners who might be passing by. When Stephenson heard about the wedding, within hours, he approached the priest on that front porch and shot Fr. Coyle, killing him instantly. Several people passing by would have seen this take place. The minister then went to the courthouse to state that he had just killed a priest.

The funeral of Fr. Coyle was the largest funeral that Birmingham had ever had. Hundreds of people attended from all over. At the trial, several members of the jury were KKK members. A witness to the murder was not allowed to testify. Pastor Stephenson pleaded not guilty by reason of insanity, for he declared that his daughter's marriage to a Catholic had driven him insane. The judge and jury foreman were members of the Klan. The Klan hired and paid for Stephenson's lawyer, the future Supreme Court Judge, Hugo Black. Stephenson was declared not guilty.

After the death of Fr. Coyle, the KKK lost favor among the people. [32]

Forces Going After the Klan

Eventually, state legislatures and national organizations began organizing forces against the Klan's existence. In an attempt to keep the Klan from operating in the state of Nebraska, it passed legislation on January 23, 1923, with certain prohibitions meant to keep the Klan out: specifically, it "prohibited non-law enforcing persons, singly or collectively, from imposing or administering penalties for alleged infractions, and places a barrier on sacred meetings for the purpose of carrying out threats or making investigations." [33]

---

[32] "Remembering James Coyle: The Irish Priest the Ku Klux Klan Killed," James Wilson @JamesWilson1919, July 20, 2022.

[33] "Anti-Klan Bill Passed in Nebraska," *The Southern Messenger*, February 1, 1923.

[34] Fr. James A. Coyle (1873-1921)
Irish Priest Who stood up to the Klan

[34] Fr. James A. Coyle (1873-1921), Irish Priest Who stood up to the Klan, Find a Grave.com.

In the latter part of 1923, the National Vigilance Association was formed. The explicit purpose was to organize a country-wide campaign to fight the Klan. Headquarters were opened in Washington, D.C. The *Dallas News*, which reported the development, stated that the group consisted of men prominent in the educational, business, and professional life from around the country. The group had in mind the passing of an anti-masking bill in every state legislature, the bringing of sufficient influence on state legislatures to compel secret organizations to reveal their membership rosters, the establishment of a federal statute to cover mob violence and provide federal protection of offenders, among other measures. [35]

The American Federation of Labor meeting in Portland, Oregon, denounced the Klan in its executive report. It referred to the KKK for its "usurpation of government." It called upon all trade unionists to beware of the Klan. [36]

Within the city of Amarillo, in Texas, T.W. Stanford, a Klansman, was found guilty in a district court on the charge of whitecapping. He was sentenced to two years in prison. This was the first guilty verdict because of the flogging of a Mr. McDonald. Charges of assault with a prohibited weapon have not been brought forth. Lieutenant Governor T.W. Davidson, the acting governor, began the

---

[35] "Anti-Klan Body Organized at Washington, National Vigilance Association to Combat Invisible Empire," *The Southern Messenger*, November 22, 1923.

[36] "Klan Denounced by Labor Federation," Convention Declares Kluxers Menace to Government," *Southern Messenger, October 11, 1923.*

investigation when it was apparent that county officials would not move forward. The sheriff and county attorney were indicted. [37]

Leading to Justice

It is important to bear in mind that the federal and state governments involved do prosecute KKK offenders when they have the evidence to do so. Patrick Scanlan, former Managing Editor of the *Brooklyn Tablet,* followed up on D.C. Stephenson, the former grand dragon of the Ku Klux Klan in Indiana. He began simply as a salesman for membership. He was able to pocket one-third of the $10.00 membership fee. He enrolled 200,000 men by 1925. In 1925, his personal wealth was estimated at $984,000. He promoted the sale of *The Fiery Cross,* plus other KKK materials. He became the grand dragon for 21 Midwestern states, which became another source of income. He lived in a large home in Indianapolis, possessing his own yacht, plane, and bodyguards. He controlled the Indiana state legislature. He actually assaulted a State House secretary, Madge Oberholtzer. His bodyguards took her to a house owned by D.C. She died a few weeks later, but had released a statement to physicians stating that Stephensen had "brutally assaulted her." Stephensen was convicted of second-degree murder as he had withheld medical attention from his victim. He was in prison for thirty years. Released at age 65, he

[37] "Wearing Robes of Klan Held Criminal: Texas Klansman Sentenced to Two Years' Imprisonment," *Southern Messenger*, October 18, 1923.

was told to leave the state of Indiana and not to return. So, he was influential with the Klan, but it cost him dearly in the end. [38]

Unfortunately, hearings were opened in reference to the murder of two men, Watt Daniels and Thomas Richards. These two individuals had publicly opposed the Klan. The KKK "intimidated" local officials following the murder, which created a disposition such that little action was taken. State and Federal officials were involved in the investigation. The bodies of the two men were drawn from the waters of Lake, La. Two men have confessed to their role in the murder of the two men. The confessions of these men implicate forty-five men. These confessions provide the story of the kidnapping of five citizens of Mer Rouge. One was released. Two were whipped. Daniels and Richards were tortured and put to death [39]. The Klan members expected to mistreat these two men, perhaps disfigure them, but not assassinate them. They were probably killed as a result of "developments on the scene." Daniel recognized the Klansmen. The KKK knew Daniel to be a man of courage, who would not rest with the "indignities placed upon them." Thus, the murders followed. It was not uncommon for the practice of "selling out" to take place after such murders—those who were called forth as witnesses could find themselves sold out before the trial. Harold Tegerstrom, a 19-year-old worker for a carbon company, has been named as a government witness against T.J. Burnett, one of the men charged

---

[38] Patrick Scanlan, K.S.C, "Man of the Past: Former Grand Dragon of the K.K.K.," *Brooklyn Tablet*, January 24, 1957.

[39] "Forty-Five Men Implicated in Mer Rouge Murder. Authorities Said to be in Possession of Details of Kidnapping and Killing," *Southern Messenger*, January 4, 1923.

with the murder of Daniels and Richards. Sadly, Tegerstrom is currently missing from the scene. Four units of the State National Guard were placed in the area to prevent further violence.[40] To their dismay, members of the KKK attempted to blame the Knights of Columbus for these acts. Of course, the Knights would not accept such slander.[41]

The Klan's scope broadened over time. It extended far beyond the lives and liberties of Catholics, Jews, and Negroes. In the January issue (1923) of Hearst's International magazine, the editor announced that they would attempt to control the courts, the legislatures, and the national government. A group called the Imperial Klan would attempt to enroll politicians, judges, and other prominent individuals. Dr. W. H. Evans, then the new Imperial Wizard, stated that he was sending agents to Washington, D.C., to spread the influence of the Klan.[42]

It is also very noteworthy that the fight against the Klan was met on several fronts. Protestant groups have banded together to form the American Unity League. Their membership received letters from across the country expressing great opposition to the Klan. They hear that the KKK is attempting to tear down institutions established by this country 140 years ago, specifically equal rights, freedom, and the separation of Church and State. They recognize that the Klan is using funds obtained in the East to win elections in

---

[40] "Violence Feared If Klan Lawlessness Exposed-Hearing Opens to Probe Killings in Mer Rouge," *Southern Messenger*, January 11, 1923.

[41] "Knights of Columbus," *The Southern Messenger*, February 22, 1923.

[42] "The Real Menace of the Klan," *The Southern Messenger*, January 4, 1923.

the South.[43] The American Unity League realized that an effective weapon in fighting the Klan was a publication of the officers and members of the Klan. This was done in Chicago, leading to the resignation of members of the Klan. These individuals have lost business, been ostracized, and lost friends. The publication "Tolerance" refers to it as "Pulling the hoods off."[44] Members of the Lafayette Klan voted to disband. However, they did not perceive themselves as anti-Jewish or anti-Catholic; Catholics and Jews did. Thus, according to the *New Orleans Times -Picayune*, they voted at a special meeting to disband. Unrest had come about due to a pamphlet distributed with the names of all members of the Lafayette, Louisiana Klan.[45]

The *Houston Chronicle* reported on June 4, 1923, the formation of women's groups of the KKK. This group claimed formation through five large Protestant bodies. The women themselves stated they had a starting membership of 260,000. The formation of this group of 260,000 was in opposition to a women's group that had existed for some time, the Knights of the White Kamelia.[46] However, it needs to be pointed out that the League of Protestant Women wished to have nothing to do with the Ku Klux Klan. They declared they would maintain their own sovereignty in women's secret

---

[43] "Protestants Will Fight the Ku Klux Klan – To Maintain American Institutions and Principles As Established 140 Years Ago," *The Southern Messenger*, August 31, 1922.

[44] Chicago's Campaign against the Ku Klux – Publication of members' Names Leads to Resignations," *The Southern Messenger*, October 12, 1922.

[45] "Lafayette Klan Disbands," *Southern Messenger*, April 12, 1923.

[46] "Kamelia" Has Strong Opposition – New Women's Ku Klux Klan Organized in Washington," *The Southern Messenger*, June 14, 1923.

circles. [47] Again, this illustrates the divisions existing within and beyond the Klan.

Within a small town in Texas, robed Klansmen walked in after the congregation had sung a hymn. The leader of the group of ten Klansmen then, disguising his voice, said a prayer and gave the minister an envelope. The minister was amazed at the interruption, saying he did not want to be disturbed. The elders and deacons of the Church of Christ stated they did not believe in the practices of the KKK and thus returned the envelope containing $15.00 to the masked men. [48]

Within a meeting of the Elks held in Chicago, the governor of the state of Louisiana, John Parker, stated that the KKK had just as much right to organize as any other group, but not to "transcend" the laws of this society. Meanwhile, the Illinois legislature passed a bill imposing longer prison sentences and heavier fines when the "perpetrators" are masked. [49]

In the meantime, the American Federation of Labor at its convention denounced "the usurpation of government by the Klan." It referred to the KKK as a menace to the American Government. The proposal was unanimously passed. [50]

---

[47] League of Protestant Women Declines to Affiliate with the Ku Klux Klan," *The Southern Messenger*, June 21, 1923.

[48] "Klansmen Interrupt Religious Services-Intruders Rebuked by Minister," *The Southern Messenger, July 26, 1923.*

[49] "Klan Criminals Should Be Punished, Governor Parker Says," *The Southern Messenger*, July 5, 1923.

[50] "Klan Denounced by Labor Federation," *The Southern Messenger*, October 11, 1923.

The State of Texas scored a victory when an alleged Klansman was found guilty in a district court of whitecapping. He was sentenced to two years in the state prison. Charges of assault with a prohibited weapon have not been tried. The county officials were not disposed to proceed. The sheriff and county attorney were indicted. [51]

Unfortunately, some members of the KKK chose to spread their poisonous propaganda among the officers of the reserve list of the army and navy. Efforts were made to spread Klan broadcasts throughout the American Army. The War Department itself was opposed to any affiliation of members of the army or any other branch of service with the Klan. This was also true of the Chairman of the Senate Committee on Military Affairs. Lucrative rewards were promised to those who peddled KKK propaganda. Fortunately, individuals who found themselves caught up in this web said they could not serve the "Emperor" of the Klan and be faithful to their country. In other words, patriotism professed a much higher calling than that of the Klan. These attempts have now been publicized and these new KKK members have been allowed to rethink their decision. [52] Fr. Francis Duffy, a wartime chaplain, was to address the 165

---

[51] "Wearing Robes of Klan Held Criminal: Texas Klansman Sentenced to Two Years' Imprisonment," *The Southern Messenger, October 18, 1923.*

[52] "Ku Klux Attempt to Invade American Army 'No Divided Allegiance Will be Permitted,' Says Chairman of Senate Committee on Military Affairs," *The Southern Messenger*, August 24, 1922.

Regiment at a memorial service. The KKK tried to keep him off the program, but the committee spokesman refused.[53]

In 1922, the Board of Directors of the Ancient Order of Hibernians saw the KKK as attempting to create division among the American people. The movement is further against Irish American Catholics, as no other group of Catholics is so prominent in America. Irish American Catholics are known for their "aggressive citizenship."[54] Three years later, in 1925, the President of the Ancient Order of the Hibernians had as its purpose the promotion of the group at the Annual Convention. He discussed several topics at the Convention. Still, he gave great attention to the denunciation of the KKK, stating that they could woo foreign agencies in an effort to drag America into aligning with the forces of imperialism. He described the Klan as "perhaps the most un-Christian, the most baneful influence in America today."[55]

Discord eventually appeared within and beyond the Klan, leading to its demise. Dr. W.H. Evans of Dallas, a long-time Klan leader, was not able to convince Governor Henry J. Allen of Kansas of the value of a so-called reform group dressed in disguise. The Governor objected basically to its "clandestine" activities. He believed its members were carrying out "private grudges" behind a mask.[56]

---

[53] "Fr. Duffy Addresses Rainbow Veterans-Despite Klan Protest," *The Southern Messenger,* August 9, 1923.

[54] "Ancient Order of Hibernians," – Ku Klux Klan Denounced by Board of Directors," *The Southern Messenger,* August 17, 1922.

[55] "President Coolidge Lauds Work of A.O.H. in Letter," *The Southern Messenger,* July 30, 1925.

[56] "Governor Allen Not Converted by Dr. Evans-Determined to Drive Klan Out of Kansas," *Southern Messenger,* December 28, 1922.

In another account of friction within the Klan leadership, Captain J.K. Skipwith, "exalted cyclops" of the Morehouse Parish KKK, was asked to resign and leave the state by members of the Klan from Morehouse, Madison, and Ouachita parishes. Skipwith had been involved in defending the Klan against the state's investigation. Skipwith refused to leave the state or resign. Whether Skipwith would remain in office is determined by the "outcome of a battle between the Evans and Simmons factions within the Klan. It is reported that Evans favors the resignation of Skipwith, and Simmons wished him to remain in office. Skipwith has gone to Atlanta, the Klan's headquarters. There, he discovered that the records of the Klan investigation into Morehouse Parish, in addition to a proclamation ousting Skipwith, had disappeared.

Two Klan meetings were held in San Antonio, as it appeared. The Imperial Wizard, Dr. W.H. Evans, became the leader of those who remained faithful to him. George W. Keeling chaired another hastily convened meeting, as it was apparent that Evans no longer accepted him. Thus, followers of Keeling drew together an impromptu meeting. It appears there would be a widening of the breach between two separate Klans. Further, the "Emperor" William Joseph Simmons was supposed to address Klansmen and their wives Saturday night. [57]

The Atlanta Baptists Ministers' Conference, composed of pastors of over one hundred Baptist churches in the Atlanta area, went on record objecting to the continuance of Dr. C.A. Ridley's ministry

---

[57] 'The Battle Royal Is On – Kleagle of Texas Klan Is "Fired" by Evans,' *The Southern Messenger*, June 23, 1923.

as a chaplain of the Ku Klux Klan. They saw Ridley's association as "an injury to the cause of Christ and a reflection upon the honor of Baptists." This group of Baptist ministers stated they would appeal to the Atlanta Association of Baptist churches. The Baptist ministers disclaimed ecclesiastical authority but asserted they must "disavow any further responsibility for the fellowship which our common ordination vows have created." Ridley chose to wrap himself in an American flag as he came to the end of his talks attacking the Catholic Church. [58]

M. Charles D. McGehee, formerly a pastor of a Methodist Episcopal Church in St. Louis, had served as a Klan lecturer. He was appointed a First Lieutenant in the US Officers' Reserve to serve as a chaplain. The American Legion demanded that he resign from the position.

Within the state of New York, members of the Klan objected to the Walker law, which the state legislature passed in 1923. The KKK must reveal its members' names. When the Klan objected, the *New York Times* and *The New York World* printed strong editorial condemnations of the Klan, stating that members should be arrested and brought to trial. [59]

Judge Preston Reynolds of Dallas, who was a life member of the KKK, came to Houston on May 23, 1923, as a representative of William Joseph Simmons. Simmons was the founder and emperor of the Knights of the Invisible Empire. Reynolds' mission in Houston

---

[58] "Ku Klux Pastor Scored by Baptists-Ministers' Conference Condemns Acts of Dr. C.A. Ridley," *The Southern Messenger, June 21, 1923.*

[59] "New York Newspapers Warn Klansmen Not to Attempt to Defy Law," *The Southern Messenger*, June 7, 1923.

was to "clean up" the Klan. He referred to naming individuals to high office in the Klan who had terrible criminal records in America. He referred to the use of Klan funds for the "subsidizing of the dirtiest little sheets that ever disgraced the name of journalism."[60]

Protestants within the state of Virginia, specifically Norfolk, showed great concern over the kidnapping of Fr. Vincent D. Warren by masked, robed, and armed men. After the incident, the city council passed an ordinance outlawing the wearing of masks within the city. Within the two weeks since the kidnapping, it is believed that 28 hooded men kidnapped Fr. Warren. It was further thought that the kidnapping was planned and that individuals from Norfolk did it. The identity of at least two of the individuals was known.[61]

Happily, on the recommendation of a member and acceptance of remaining members, the Ku Klux Klan of Brenham, Texas, disbanded as of July 21, 1924.[62]

When addressing the issue of American ideals of the Ku Klux Klan, the *Wall Street Journal* said there are no American ideals within the KKK. This statement was further stated in *The New York Tribune*. It went on to state that there are no ideals higher than the Ten Commandments. Rather, there is nothing that has done more

---

[60] "Ku Klux Klan Strongly Denounced by Judge Reynolds of Dallas, 'Life' Member of Klan," *The Southern Messenger*, May 31, 1923.

[61] "Virginia Protestants Condemn the Kidnapping of Father V.D. Warren," *Southern Messenger*, September 23, 1926. 126

[62] "Brenham Ku Klux Klan Disbands on Motion of Barney Parker," Circular Distributed over Washington County, Texas.

harm than the KKK within the past ten years. The duty, therefore, is to disband from this organization. [63]

As 1924 approached, Klan membership further declined. Approximately 2,800,000 individuals voted to withdraw from the Klan, citing dissatisfaction with the current leadership of the Klan. The leadership was accused of not "playing fair" with the membership. This information came from D.C. Stephenson, who was head of the propaganda department for the States. The matter had been put to a vote in various states. [64]

Within the state of Texas, specifically, Houston, the Catholic Truth Society is fighting a revival of the Klan through the literature they are handing out in outlying districts. The Catholic Truth Society is fighting the same falsehoods that have been propagated in earlier times. The anti-Klan element in Texas is warned to be on guard. Requests have been coming into the Catholic Truth Society for accurate information on Catholic beliefs. [65]

The KKK and Monsignor James Kirwin

Monsignor Kirwin was an outspoken critic of the Klan. There is no wonder they wished to go after him. Yet he could deliver a

---

[63] "Only Duty of Klan Is to Disband at Once – Says *Wall Street Journal* in Recent Editorial," *The Southern Messenger,* October 11, 1923.

[64] "2,800,000 Klansmen withdraw from Organization – Members Express Dissatisfaction of Present Administration," *The Southern Messenger,* January 10, 1924.

[65] P.L. McGreal, "Truth Society A Big Factor in Thwarting Revival of the Klan in Outlying Districts," *The Southern Messenger*, July 2, 1925.

message against the Klan without mentioning that verbiage. One commonly knows of their prejudice against certain groups of people. Thus, in his sermons, he brought forth the evil that prejudice can bring about, as he stated below that there is no place for prejudice:

No Place for Prejudice

Blind prejudice is likely to undermine national unity.

Too many of us confound liberty and license, freedom and independence.

"As free and not making liberty a cloak for malice, but as servants of God, honor all men." Tendencies to question the loyalty of anybody because of racial or religious differences must not manifest themselves.....Insidious rumor and implied disloyalty can destroy the unity and harmony of this republic,....we invariably find personal prejudice, "the cloak of malice."

It seems one would wish to guard against prejudice after hearing such a message. Note the destruction it causes, which is quite evident around one, then and today.

Monsignor was quick to say that we are called to replace any whisper of prejudice with truth. [66]

He encouraged all to be slow to speak. If that had been the case, he thought, the situation in World War I could have been avoided. We have been "begotten by the word of truth" (James 1:18).

---

[66] Fr. James Kirwin, "No Place for Prejudice," *Memoirs of Monsignor J.M. Kirwin.* George T. Elmendorf, Compiler, n.d.

Protection of the Holy Spirit will teach all truth. The Church loves the epistle of James and reads it to her children. However, we are quick to speak yet somewhat slow to hear.[67] Unfortunately, the Klan in Houston infiltrated the American Legion. In 1921, a war memorial flagpole was placed at the corner of Main and McKinney. The Klan saw this as an opportunity and thus donated a flag to be flown from this flagpole. Monsignor had no intention of saluting the flag on the corner of Main and McKinney Streets, for that American flag had been given by the Ku Klux Klan. Kirwin was very familiar with the allegiance owed to the American flag, as he had been an active member of military groups for much of his adult life. He further came from members of his family who had fought under the flag.[68] Monsignor Kirwin had inherited a deeper love for his country than his attempted persecutors. He came from a stock that fought under the '61 flag. Every Galvestonian who left for Cuba from Cathedral Hall in '98 knew that their soldier chaplain was Fr. James Kirwin. This was evident even though the foe at that time was the Catholic country of Spain. An outstanding war worker during World War I was Monsignor Kirwin. General John Pershing personally called for him. Even though he had gotten as far as New York, he graciously turned back to tend to business in the diocese of Galveston due to the ill health of Bishop Gallagher.[69]

---

[67] Fr. James Kirwin, "Be Slow to Speak," *Memoirs of Monsignor J.M. Kirwin.* George T. Elmendorf, Compiler, n.d.

[68] Moore, 67.

[69] Stephen P. Brown, Student of the Monsignor, "Monsignor James M. Kirwin," *Memoirs of Monsignor J.M. Kirwin* George T. Elmendorf, Compiler,

When the American dead returned from their battlefields to their Church and their country, the government judged them to have the highest military honors. Such was the case of a Catholic young man. His flag-draped coffin was carried through the streets of Houston, accompanied by a military escort, to pay the final farewell. At the cemetery in the midst of the hushed quiet at the end of the ceremony, Fr. Kirwin stood to say, "This day, for the first time in my life, I passed an American flag and did not uncover my head because that flag had a dirty spot." As a result of this statement, people realized what the KKK was doing. Monsignor James Kirwin traveled almost daily between the Seminary in LaPorte and the Cathedral in Galveston. He had been an outspoken critic of the Klan for some time. Accordingly, Monsignor Klan was on the list of the KKK to be tarred and feathered. The plan was to abduct him when he got off the night train in LaPorte for this tar and feathering. [70] Fr. Kirwin's life was in danger. Individuals were waiting for Fr. Kirwin when he got off the train in LaPorte. These were all non-Catholics, and each was carrying a rifle. The "armed delegation" escorted him to the seminary. Fortunately, the plot on his life, the plot to tar and feather him, was never carried out. [71]

Oliver Allstorm was a very active member of the Klan in Houston. He actually wrote a pamphlet attacking Monsignor James Kirwin entitled "The Priest and the Flag." It was extensively circulated across the country by the propaganda agencies of the Klan.

---

[70] Ibid.

[71] Moore, 145 and Stephen P. Brown, Student of the Monsignor, "Monsignor James M. Kirwin," *Memoirs of Monsignor J.M. Kirwin*, George T. Elmendorf, Compiler,

Fortunately, Mr. Allstorm, a former Klan lecturer, came to his senses and retired from the KKK. [72]

Monsignor Kirwin saw only one symbol he would give greater reverence to than the American flag, and that is the cross representing the Roman Catholic Church. This 100% American was attempting to teach Americanism to this un-American organization. [73]

---

[72] P.D. McGreal, "Ku Klux Klan Scathingly Denounced by Oliver Allstrom, Former Klan Lecturer Asserts Hooded Organization Rapidly Disintegrating in Texas." *Southern Messenger*, November 1, 1923.

[73] "Kirwin and the Klan," Holdings of Rosenberg Library, Galveston, TX.

Chapter Six

Addresses of Monsignor James Kirwin

Bishop Gallagher and Fr. Kirwin

Certainly, history illustrates that Bishop Gallagher and Fr. Kirwin worked very well together over several years. In an age long before computers, televisions, and other electronic media, those who were gifted as great speakers could certainly be well occupied in providing presentations for various events. Such was the case not long after the Civil War, when great battles or other well-known military events were recalled. Kirwin was one of those gifted individuals.[1]

Not long after the 1900 storm, specifically on September 27, Bishop Gallagher celebrated Mass and invested postulants with the habit. The "golden-tongued" Fr. Kirwin preached on the text, "He who puts his hand to the plow and looks back is not fit for the kingdom of heaven."[2]

---

[1]James Talmadge Moore, *Acts of Faith: The Catholic Church in Texas, 1900-1950* (College Station, Texas: Texas A & M University Press, 2002), 5-6.

[2] Sr. Loyola Hegarty, CCVI, *Serving with Gladness, The Origin and History of the Congregation of the Sisters of Charity of the Incarnate Word, Houston, Texas* (Houston, Texas: Bruce Publishing in cooperation with the Sisters of Charity of the Incarnate Word. Houston, Texas, 1967), 332.

Bishop Gallagher laid the cornerstone in the presence of a group of local and visiting clergy on April 9, 1901, for the convent and chapel of St. Mary's Infirmary.[3]

Dedication of the New Organ at St. Mary's Cathedral

When Msgr. Kirwin arrived in the Diocese of Galveston in 1896, and Bishop Gallagher immediately appointed him as rector of St. Mary's Cathedral in Galveston. As the Cathedral for the diocese, St. Mary's was a busy parish. When the new organ arrived in 1921, Msgr. Kirwin gave the dedicatory address. He chose to illustrate the organ's magnificence by noting its intricate role in the life of the individual.

He saw the development of the organ as the story of man's effort to reach by art the mind and soul of his fellow man.

Msgr. Kirwin referred to Alexandria as a great commercial center. It was the time when the Old Testament was being translated from Hebrew to Greek. Ctesibius of Alexandria, a physicist and inventor, created what became known as a hydraulus. It was an effort to make pipes serve musically. "The process of compressing the air that a reservoir might be had was accomplished by setting a bell shaped instrument down into a large tank of water." [4]

It appealed greatly to listeners, including Cicero. Not until the eighteenth century was the instrument improved. Interestingly, the

---

[3] Ibid., 334

[4] "Dedication of New Organ. Father Kirwin's Address," *Southern Messenger*, October 6, 1921.

Latin Vulgate translated a verse in the psalms, "Laudate eum in choris et organo."

The organ for St. Mary's was the "heart's desire" of Fr. Chataignon. His love for music had led him to develop the boys' voices and manly character in the parish. He had really desired a choir which could sing "becomingly and artistically" in the service of the Divine Master. A special thanks was extended to Fr. Chataignon, the assistant pastor at the Cathedral, in the name of the Bishop of the diocese and the parishioners of the Cathedral parish.

Anthony Rahe was seen as an artist who had lent enthusiasm to his efforts. The selections contributed by Rahe, the organist of the Cathedral, were recognized as "particularly pleasing, emphasizing the ability of the artist and bringing out the tones of the organ itself." These included, in part, Ave Maria Stella, rendered by a vocal trio. Special mention was given to individual numbers.

Due to the inclement weather, the recital with the new organ was presented twice. [5]

St. Mary's Cathedral was indeed appreciative of Msgr. Kirwin, in his contributions to the parish through his speaking abilities, as illustrated by the notice provided to the parishioners when Msgr. Kirwin was going to give an address.

---

[5] Ibid.

NOTE.

To Congregation:

Father Kirwin is giving on Sunday nights at Benediction a course of instructions on fundamental principles of religion, that are, indeed, worthy of your recognition.

His sermons are homilies and wholesome and have none of the bitterness of controversy. They are not polemics, but instructions. They disclose vast reading and profound and vigorous thought and are masterpieces of eloquent address.

We recommend that you attend Benediction and hear the sermon each Sunday evening at 7:30.

And we request that you perform your lay duty by bringing some one with you.

At a time when many millions in other countries are in the throes of war you should be zealous and encourage religion and attend religious ceremonies, with the intention of gratitude and thanksgiving that we are at peace with the world, and pray that universal peace may soon ensue.

BOARD OF MANAGERS

[6]

Silver Jubilee of Ordination to the Priesthood (1895-1920)

The Silver Jubilee of Ordination of Fr. James Kirwin was held on June 23, 1920. A High Mass was celebrated in the Cathedral with Fr. Meara as the Arch Priest, Msgr. James Kelly serving as Deacon and Fr. Joseph Valenta as Subdeacon.

Within the Sanctuary, His Grace, Archbishop Shaw of New Orleans, Bishop Byrne, Bishop Lynch, Bishop Van de Ven, and Bishop Allen were present, along with four Monsignori and 55 priests from Texas and other states.

[6] Courtesy of Rosenberg Library.

St. Mary's Cathedral in Galveston, built by
Bishop John Odin, C.M., in 1847. Our Lady, Star of the Sea,
ushers sailors into the port of Galveston. It is a minor Basilica.

A banquet was held at the Hotel Galvez at 1:00 pm. Archbishop Shaw of New Orleans gave the Invocation.

The following toasts were given with Marion Douglas as the Toastmaster:

"Fr. Kirwin as a Citizen" Hon. Mart H. Roydon

"Fr. Kirwin as a Soldier and a Patriot" Capt. Will C. Lothrop

"Fr. Kirwin as a Friend" Col. Robert G. Street

"Fr. Kirwin as an Instructor" P.J. Donoghue

"Fr. Kirwin as a Priest" Rt. Rev. C. E. Byrne

Response by the Guest of Honor, Rev. Father James M. Kirwin, V.G.

During the evening within the Galveston Auditorium, "a great demonstration of love and respect" was shown to the Jubilarian. Mr. Sam Williams served as chairman and called upon speakers to represent the various professions. Mayor H. S. Sappington recognized Fr. Kirwin as the "foremost citizen" of Galveston. Mr. Kempner referred to him as a friend of mankind. Chas. J. Stubbs spoke in the name of the Cathedral Parish, attributing to him the qualities of a good Pastor. He held up a picture of Fr. Kirwin while speaking. Several patriotic and Irish songs were rendered; Fr. Kirwin then addressed the group, which was the climax of the evening. Music during the evening was provided by the Hotel Galvez Orchestra.

[7] Dignitaries and Officers of the Jubilee Mass held at St. Mary's Cathedral, Galveston, Texas, June 23, 1920, on the occasion of the Silver Jubilee of Very Reverend James M. Kirwin, V.G.

---

[7] Dignitaries and Officers of the Jubilee Mass held at St. Mary's Cathedral, Galveston, Texas, June 23, 1920, on the occasion of the Silver Jubilee of Very Reverend James M. Kirwin, V.G., *Memoirs of Monsignor James Kirwin*, George T. Elmendorf, Compiler, n.p.

[8] Chalice gifted to Very Reverend James Kirwin on the Silver Jubilee of his priestly ordination.

[8] Chalice gifted to Very Reverend James Kirwin on the Silver Jubilee of his priestly ordination. Courtesy of St. Mary's Seminary.

Msgr Kirwin on Pope Leo XIII

Pope Leo XIII passed away on July 20, 1903. This pontiff was well known for his writing, including the following encyclicals: *Providentissimus Deus, Aeterni Patris, Rerum Novarum*, and *Immortale Dei.*

A Solemn Pontifical Mass in St. Mary's Cathedral was offered on July 21, 1903. Bishop Gallagher officiated at the Mass. The diocese's clergy were in attendance. The faithful gathered to give reverence to the memory of the Pontiff. The Cathedral was decorated with gold and white streamers, the papal colors. A catafalque bearing the coat of arms of the Pope and a bust of Leo XIII was placed directly in front of the chancel at the end of the center aisle.

Msgr. Kirwin gave a biographical sketch and then his own reflections on the Pontiff. He chose to preach on the passage:

"Behold, a great priest who in his days pleased God and was found just. There has been found none like him."

Msgr. Kirwin stated that his personal reflections were like a benediction.

He experienced "positive filial affections" for the Pontiff, coupled with sentiments of personal veneration and great admiration for his intellect. He recalled the tall, slightly bent, aged figure as he stood to receive Msgr. Kirwin and those who were with him. He recalled his firm, deep, melodious voice. His face was as bloodless as a marble statue. His keen eyes had lost the fire and intensity of youth. His trembling hand was held above ours in benediction. One forgot his feebleness and age in his presence. He was quick to ask questions and thoroughly comprehended each detail. He possessed a great solicitude for the Church in America. He showed a keen interest in Galveston's disaster. His fatherly and kind farewell and benediction would live on with Msgr. Kirwin.[9]

The Church certainly mourned the loss of Pope Leo XIII, yet the Master Himself guides the boat of Peter "to the consummation of the world."

His Holiness Pope Leo XIII[10]

---

[9]*Memoirs of Monsignor J.M. Kirwin*, George T. Elmendorf, Compiler, n p.

[10]His Holiness Pope Leo XIII, Denver Register.org, and *Memoirs of Monsignor J.M. Kirwin*, George T. Elmendorf, Compiler, n p.

[11] Right Rev. Nicholas Gallagher, D.D, Consecrated Titular Bishop Of Canopus, April 30. 1882: Succeeded to Galveston December 16, 1892; Died January 21, 1918

---

[11] Right Rev. Nicholas Gallagher, D.D, Consecrated Titular Bishop of Canopus, April 30. 1882: Succeeded to Galveston December 16, 1892; Died January 21, 1918, *Memoirs of Monsignor J.M. Kirwin.* George Elmendorf, Compiler, n. p.

Dedication of St. Joseph Infirmary

The dedication of St. Joseph Infirmary in Galveston took place on May 8, 1919. Msgr. James Kirwin had been asked to give the address.

According to tradition, the first Bishop of Limoges, St. Martial, was blessed by the Savior Himself and shown to be His disciple.

Jeanne de Matel received her inspiration to establish the Sisters of the Incarnate Word and Blessed Sacrament in Lyon, France, in 1625. As a member of the French School, she adopted much of that spirituality. Unfortunately, she suffered tremendous persecution during her lifetime, which may have hastened her death in 1670. There was a century of intense persecution of the Catholic religion, ending in the French Revolution. The Order "walked in the land of desolation and exile until the French Revolution itself had spent itself" [12] in its own excesses and sought the grace of God again.

In 1852, the Sisters of the Incarnate Word and Blessed Sacrament began educating poor children and caring for the sick in Texas. Bishop Odin, the first Bishop of Texas, with the consent of the Holy See, requested that Sisters come to Texas for education. Some years later, in 1866, Bishop Dubuis, the second Bishop of Texas, visited the convent in Lyon and asked that the Sisters come to Texas to care for the sick and orphaned. Their ministry began in Galveston. Specifically, Sr. Mary Blandine, Sr. Mary Joseph, and Sr. Mary Ange launched their new ministry at 8th and Market Street in Galveston. They became known as the Sisters of Charity of the Incarnate Word.

---

[12] Fr. James Kirwin, "Dedication of St. Joseph's Infirmary," *Memoirs of Monsignor J.M. Kirwin.* George T. Elmendorf, Compiler, n.p.

In scarcely half a century, the Sisters expanded the hospital network to Beaumont, Lake Charles, Shreveport, Texarkana, Alexandria, and Temple. These hospitals all fell under the Motherhouse in Galveston. Bishop Dubuis believed that due to distance, a second Congregation should begin in San Antonio with the same mission. This followed promptly and likewise flourished in its care for the sick.

In 1887, Rev. Thomas Hennessy, pastor of Annunciation Church in Houston, requested, with the approval of Bishop Gallagher, that the Sisters of Charity of the Incarnate Word open a small hospital in Houston. This was accomplished through a two-story wooden structure on the corner of Caroline and Franklin Streets. Mother St. Louis and Mother Theresa were the first Sisters to begin this ministry. A 100-bed hospital was opened in 1895 on Crawford Street, with subsequent expansion.

Msgr. Kirwin did not intend to give a history of St. Joseph Infirmary. Rather, he pointed out their heroic endeavors in the smallpox epidemic in 1890 and 1891, the fire in 1894 through which Sr. Doloretta and her companion lost their lives, and the ten Sisters who drowned in the 1900 storm, in addition to the ninety orphans. [13]

He closed by noting, "And in our love your service shall avail, so that the very stars shall fade before St. Joseph's light grows pale." [14]

---

[13] Ibid.

[14] Ibid.

[15] St. Joseph's Infirmary, Houston, Texas

The Storm of 1900

Fr. Kirwin delivered this address to express appreciation for all the people who did for Galveston. He referred specifically to Psalm 139: "Out of the depths I have cried unto Thee, hear oh! Hear my prayer." He noted Rachel's cry in the Old Testament, for she wailed over her lost children. "And would not be comforted because they were not," yet there were those who survived and needed to be cared for.

Thus, the cry arose and was answered. It is as if the psalm were ringing across the wires. Thus, aid arrived from Houston: "Even though Houston was wounded herself, she forgot her own grief;

---

[15] St. Joseph's Infirmary, Houston, Texas, Houston Time Portal. *Memoirs of Monsignor J.M. Kirwin.* George T. Elmendorf, Compiler, n.p.

once a rival, now an admiration, came immediate succor and relief." As Fr. Kirwin stated, Houston was once seen as an opponent. Thus, Houston "forgot her own grief; merged them in our greater sorrow and lifted the burden of stricken Galveston that she might rise to her feet, and once the footing was gained, the sturdy, strong heroic sons and tender merciful daughters of Galveston lent themselves to a task that far surpassed the former griefs of humankind." [16] Special trains thundered south, bringing food and angels who ministered to the broken hearts in whatever way possible.

One could never forget "the teeming morgues! The heavily freighted death barges! The funeral pyres! Shall we ever forget them? Great God, Galveston thanked Thee for these strong men and tender women, whom death could not blanch nor desolation overwhelm!" [17]

Galveston was so busy burying and burning her dead children, feeding the hungry, and clothing the naked, in each case with whatever they could find. When communication by wire and rail was restored, the state of Texas, the Governor, the Nation, and the President, in fact, "the world stood aghast at our horrors and rang with our necessities." Aid even came from across the Atlantic and the sister republics from the south. Clara Barton arrived with the Red Cross. They forgot themselves and exposed their tender, solicitous hearts. The wealthy came with their thousands. The widows and the poor came "with their mites and the little tots,...who gave up their

---

[16] "The Cataclysm of 1900," *Memoirs of Monsignor J.M. Kirwin.* George T Elmendorf, Compiler, n. p.

[17] Ibid.

dolls to her orphaned children who had lost their own in the flood." [18]

Galveston learned that the world had wept with it, and the people of Galveston were indeed thankful for their aid. "The world's charity has healed the broken heart." [19]

A message was brought to Galveston with the aid for her citizens, specifically a message of hope and confidence as found in the words of Longfellow:

Galveston! Build on, nor fear to breast the sea,
Our hearts, our hopes, are all with thee;
Our hearts, our hopes, our prayers, our tears,
Our Faith triumphant o'er our fears,
Are all with thee-are all with thee!" [20]

Building of the Seawall

To protect the city against future storms, the people of Galveston wanted a seawall built. Fr. Kirwin urged that this be done at once. Federal aid was obtained. The cornerstone was laid in 1902. Fr. Kirwin was called upon to say the prayer for the occasion. When the work was completed in 1905 and commemorative monuments were erected, Fr. Kirwin was asked to participate in the religious service, which he did.[21]

---

[18] Ibid.

[19] Ibid.

[20] Henry Wadsworth Longfellow, "The Building of the Ship" (excerpt).

[21] "Building of the Seawall," Galveston and Texas History Center.

Galveston Seawall Completed 1905

[22] Galveston Hurricane Memorial

Dedication of Newman Hall at the University of Texas in Austin, Texas, March 7th, 1918

It is most fitting that the Children of St. Dominic care for Newman Hall at the University of Texas in Austin. Bishop Gallagher had long desired that Catholic students attending a state university

[22]"Galveston Hurricane Memorial," Visit Galveston.com.

should have the Church's guiding hand in their academic endeavors. Accordingly, Bishop Gallagher had invited a religious order, the Paulist Fathers, to care for a parish in Austin while they ministered to lay students attending the University. The cornerstone was laid on March 7th, 1918, the feast of St. Thomas Aquinas. Fr. Kirwin was asked to deliver the address at that time.

The President of the University, plus members of the Holy Cross religious community, and other religious communities serving on and off campus, were in attendance. In addition, there were representatives of various Catholic organizations, including the Knights of Columbus, the Daughters of Isabella, the Society of St. Vincent de Paul, the Catholic Knights of America, and other lay Catholics. A procession began at the Newman Club. Little children from the Newman School, run by the Dominican Sisters, and Catholic University students followed. They were all chanting the solemn tones of the Miserere.

It is the Roman Catholic Church that commenced the Catholic university system that we know today. The Children of St. Dominic had imparted a legacy of culture and refinement for over seven centuries. They came to Galveston with the full approval of the late Bishop Nicholas Gallagher. The knowledge which Christ came to impart was "no mere intellectual possession or theory." Rather, "I am come that they may have life, and may have it more abundantly." Christ is "the Way, the Truth, and the Light." Certainly, Christ made provision for the perpetuation of His work by training those who would follow.

With the foundations of such Universities as Oxford, Bologna, Paris, or even as far back as Athens and Alexandria, it is evident that a revival of studies took place in the eleventh, twelfth, and, especially, the thirteenth centuries. Fr. Kirwin referred to the Middle Ages as the age of faith. The dialectical method emerged, leading to discussions of many questions at the time. This methodology led to the development of schools of law, medicine, and theology at Bologna, Salerno, and Paris.

A major part of this development stemmed from the writings of St. Thomas Aquinas (1225-1274), especially his *Summa Theologica.* This work is known today for its accuracy, its lucidity, its brevity, its power of exposition, and its universality of knowledge. It is a guiding light for training the "best disciplined body of men in the world, the clergy of the Catholic Church." [23] Leo XIII referred to the scholastic doctors of the medieval era, stating that Thomas Aquinas, who became the most venerated of the doctors of the Church, seemed, in a certain way, "to have inherited the intellect of all of them." The Pontiff referred to Aquinas as "the chief and master of all." [24]

Fr. Kirwin referred to March 7th as the anniversary of Aquinas, as it is the day of his death. The Dominican Order was actually invited into the diocese of Galveston by Bishop Gallagher. It was he who judged the necessity of their serving here in the local Church. They have served the universal Church for over seven centuries.

---

[23]Very Rev. J.M. Kirwin, "Cornerstone Laid of Newman Hall, Austin, Home for Catholic Women Students at State University," *Southern Messenger,* March 14, *1918*

[24] "Cornerstone Laid of Newman Hall, Austin, Home for Catholic Women Students at State University, to be Conducted by Dominican Sisters. History and Scope of the Work Outlined by Very Rev. J.M. Kirwin in Eloquent Address, "*Southern Messenger,* March 14, 1918.

As Catholics, Fr. Kirwin stated, we believe that Christ brought about the most important epoch of education. God spoke in times past through the prophets. He has spoken through His Son. Certainly, St Paul expresses Christ's thought. In writing to Titus, Paul reminds all that "we should live soberly and justly and piously in this world, expecting the blessed hope and coming of the great God and our Savior Jesus Christ." (Titus 2;11-12) Christ did not come for mere intellectual knowledge or theory. Rather, it was for the imparting of the great gift of faith. "I came that they may have life and may have it more abundantly" (John 10:10).

Christ brought forth the divine commission to teach, saying, "Go, therefore, teach ye all nations; teaching them to observe all things whatsoever I have commanded you and behold I am with you all days even to the consummation of the world."(Mt 28:19) These words of Christ Fr. Kirwin describes as the perpetual charter of the Catholic Church as the teaching institution. The Church must have the "greatest formative influence on all educational problems."[25] The Church is conscious of her divine mission, conscious of Christ's permanent abiding with His appointed teachers, conscious of herself as the "visible agency" through which Christ continues for all time the work He began during His lifetime on earth. The spread of His doctrine was entrusted to an organization that speaks in His name and with His authority. "As the Father has sent Me, I also send you" (John 20:21). As Fr. Kirwin emphasized, "No other body of teachers

---

[25] Very Rev. J.M. Kirwin, "Cornerstone Laid of Newman Hall, Austin, Home for Catholic Women Students at State University," *Southern Messenger,* March 14, 1918.

ever undertook such a vast work, and no other ever accomplished so much for education in the higher sense." [26]

Fr. Kirwin referred to the many tools the Catholic Church uses to teach the faith, including catechetical schools, seminaries, Catholic schools, and sermons, as provided in the various liturgies throughout the liturgical cycle. Fr. Kirwin emphasized the Church year cycle, in which she has followed Christ from the joys of the Christmas season to the desolation of Good Friday, to the triumph of Easter, and to the great confidence found in the celebration of Pentecost. Certainly, he does not forget the sanctoral cycle or the foremost honor given to Mary, the Mother of God. Referring to the liturgical cycle, the Church utilizes all of the principles which underlie great teaching, nothing new but in modern form. Fr. Kirwin emphasized the use of the senses, association, apperception, expression, and imitation.

[27] Newman Hall, Austin, TX

---

[26] Ibid.

[27] Newman Hall, Austin, TX, Austinpostcard.com.

[28] St. Thomas Aquinas, O.P. (1225-1274)

[28] St. Thomas Aquinas, O.P., 1225-1274, Catholic.org.

Advancements for Fr. James Kirwin

Fr. Kirwin was ordained to the priesthood in 1895. He arrived in the diocese of Galveston in 1896. Bishop Nicholas Gallagher immediately appointed him as rector of St. Mary's Cathedral in Galveston. He remained in that position until his death. Several years later, in 1911, Bishop Gallagher appointed him vicar general of the Diocese of Galveston in addition to serving as President of St. Mary's Seminary.

In 1922, Bishop Christopher Byrne announced that Pope Pius XI had raised Fr. Kirwin to the rank of Monsignor in recognition of his work for the Church and his patriotic service to the state and the nation. The letter was received from Cardinal De Lai in Rome in June, but the formal investiture took place in December.

At the investiture, there was an inspiring procession in which 110 members of the Fourth Degree Knights of Columbus escorted Bishop Byrne and the Rt. Rev. Monsignor Kirwin and the local and visiting clergy into the Cathedral. Several non-Catholic laymen were also present. The ecclesiastical procession entered the Church under an arch of steel, made by the drawn swords of the Knights of Columbus. The papal brief was read in Latin and then in English by Fr. Jerome Rapp, from St. Mary's Seminary.

Bishop Byrne pointed out to the Assembly that Pope Pius XI had taken notice of the distinguished career of Monsignor Kirwin. Bishop Byrne recognized the present Pope as a linguist and a scholar. He then went on to address the necessity of unity within the Church.

He referred to the words of Christ during which He prayed that the disciples might be one as Christ and the Father are one. The Bishop referred to the one fold and one shepherd. He referred to the analogy of the body as used by St. Paul. He further noted the unbroken line of popes, going back to the time of St. Peter and, as the Bishop stated, to the feet of Christ. Much must be addressed to the Popes in reference to what they have done in preserving the literature, law, art, and architecture, and the culture of the day.

The seminarians were present in the sanctuary for the following Mass. After the impressive religious service, a lovely luncheon at the Hotel Galvez included a toastmaster with toasts.

Fr. Anton J. Frank told the story of the Apostolic Delegate Pietro Cardinal Fumasoni Biondi's visit. Before Fr. Kirwin was honored, the Apostolic delegate entered the office of Fr. Kirwin and told him to close the door. Fr. Kirwin refused, stating that his life was an open book. The Apostolic Delegate then showed him a newspaper article he had clipped, in such a way as to make it appear that Fr. Kirwin paid no attention to Church teaching on cremation. Fr. Kirwin explained that, bearing in mind the dire circumstances at that time, there was no choice. The Apostolic Delegate, with sincere apology, stated that the clipping had prevented Fr. Kirwin from an elevation in rank for twenty years.[29]

---

[29] "Rt. Rev. Msgr. J.M. Kirwin, Vicar General of Galveston," *The Southern Messenger*, December 14, 1922. Fr. Anton J. Frank, Anniversary Death of Monsignor James M. Kirwin at Mass in Annunciation Church, Houston, Texas.

[30] Father James Kirwin as Domestic Prelate

[30] "Father James Kirwin as Domestic Prelate," *Memoirs of Monsignor J.M. Kirwin,* George T. Elmendorf, Compiler, n.p.

[31] Views of St.Mary's Seminary at La Porte, Texas

Views of St.Mary's Seminary at La Porte, Texas

[31] "Views of St. Mary's Seminary at La Porte, Texas," *Memoirs of Monsignor J.M. Kirwin,* George T. Elmendorf, Compiler, n.p.

Closing of Triduum at Seton Infirmary, Austin, Texas

Solemn Exercises were held at Seton Infirmary in Austin, Texas, to honor Blessed Louise de Marillac and the Blessed Martyrs of Arras. These four martyrs had died during the French Revolution, June 26, 1794, at the hands of the Guillotine as they refused to take the oath to the new government. These Sisters of Charity were beatified on June 13, 1920.

Services began in the crowded chapel on Thursday at 8:00 am for a Solemn Pontifical Mass celebrated by Rt. Rev. Christopher Byrne, D.D, Bishop of Galveston, assisted by various clergy, diocesan as well as members of religious orders. The guard of honor consisted of ten Knights of Columbus of the Fourth Degree. Other gentlemen served as the escort. The students of St. Mary's Academy provided an excellent program of sacred music during the Mass.

The sermon was given by Very Rev. J.M. Kirwin, V.G. Fr. Kirwin pointed out that St Vincent de Paul had the initial impulse to renew the diocesan clergy. In that sense, diocesan clergy today believe themselves closely aligned with his humanitarian work. Vincent de Paul was past fifty years of age when the flowering and beauty of his work was seen in the mission of the Sisters of Charity. Fr. Kirwin traced some of the more important events in the life of Louise de Marillac. The Ladies of Charity, as they were then called, came to see the necessity of serving the neglected poor. Fr. Kirwin pointed out that labor is prayer. He emphasized the scripture passage, "As often as you have done it unto the least of these My brethren you have done it unto Me." (Mt 25:40)

The streets of Paris provided a kind of cloister for Louise de Marillac and those who followed her. Fr. Kirwin referred to the modesty as their veil. Their first institution was built in Paris, which came to be known as Hotel Dieu, literally the House of God. During World War I, five thousand of these religious were on the battlefield and serving in hospitals. They were not in the rear but serving on the front lines. They were not looking for the honors of the world. The world's praise today can be the condemnations of tomorrow.

Fr. Kirwin referred to a canvas at the Louvre, painted by an artist from Texas, Seymour Thomas. It was entitled "An Innocent Victim." It portrayed a Sister of Charity who had been killed on the battlefield. At the time, Fr. Kirwin was speaking, there were forty thousand Sisters of Charity in the world, ready to make that ultimate sacrifice, if called upon. [32]

Fr. Kirwin expressed the desire that the Sisters of Charity would continue to flourish in other Texas cities "nestling like doves in your simplicity and manifesting in your humble, quiet, beneficent service to afflicted mankind the love that flamed in the earth of Jesus Christ." [33]

---

[32] Fr. James Kirwin, "Closing of Triduum at Seton Infirmary, Austin, Texas," *Memoirs of Monsignor J.M. Kirwin,* George T. Elmendorf, Compiler, n.p.

[33] Ibid.

AN INNOCENT VICTIM.
S. SEYMOUR THOMAS' MASTERPIECE.

[34]

The triduum was brought to a close with Benediction at which Bishop Byrne officiated. After Benediction, Bishop Byrne spoke briefly on the work of the Sisters of Charity. All then joined in singing the "Te Deum," followed by dinner. [35]

---

[34] "An Innocent Victim," painting of Seymour Thomas found in the Louvre.

[35] "Close of Triduum at Seton Infirmary, Austin," Solemn Exercises in Commemoration of Beatification of Five Nuns," Sou*thern Messenger*, April 14, 1921.

[36] "The Martyrs of Arras"

Diamond Jubilee of the Diocese of Galveston and St. Mary's Cathedral

This year, 1922, saw the celebration of several events. As previously stated in this volume, Fr. James Kirwin finally received the honor of Domestic Prelate. The honor was delayed due to a misunderstanding as to why bodies had to be cremated after the 1900 storm.

[36] "The Martyrs of Arras," Daughters-of-Charity.com.

It was the year of the celebration of the Diocese of Galveston and the consecration of St. Mary's Cathedral, both through the efforts of Bishop John Odin.

Booklet

Through the generous efforts of Fr. Kirwin, President of St. Mary's Seminary, an outline was provided of important milestones within the diocese of Galveston, as given below:

1840-1842
The Republic of Texas was a prefecture apostolic under the Very Reverend John Timon, C.M. It became a prefect apostolic under the Very Reverend John Mary Odin, C.M.

1842-1847
The Republic of Texas was raised from a prefecture apostolic to a vicariate apostolic, with Rt. Reverend John Mary Odin, D.D., Bishop of Claudiopolis, vicar apostolic.

1847
Erection of the diocese of Galveston took place with the Right Reverend John Mary Odin, D.D., its first bishop.

1861
In this year, following the death of Archbishop Antoine Blanc, the Right Reverend John Mary Odin, D.D., became Archbishop of New Orleans.

1862
Right Reverend C.M. Dubuis, D.D., was consecrated as Bishop of Galveston.

1874
The diocese of Galveston encompassed roughly the entire state of Texas until September 3, 1874. Following this time period, the Diocese of Galveston retained the territory east of the Colorado River. The Diocese of San Antonio was carved from the territory between the Colorado and Nueces Rivers. The Vicariate Apostolic of Brownsville was carved out of the territory between the Nueces River and the Rio Grande River.

1878
This year, the Right Reverend P. Dufal, D.D., Bishop of Delcon and Vicar Apostolic of Eastern Bengal, was transferred to Galveston as coadjutor of the Right Reverend C.D. Dubuis, *cum jure successionis*. However, he resigned in 1880.

1882
On April 30, the Right Reverend Nicholas Aloysius Gallagher was consecrated as the Titular Bishop of Canopus and Bishop Administrator of the Diocese of Galveston.

1890
The second division of the diocese of Galveston took place at the request of Bishop Gallagher. The Diocese of Dallas was created from the northern and northwestern portions of the Diocese of

Galveston. The counties of Lampasas, Coryell, McLennan, Limestone, Freestone, Anderson, Cherokee, Nacogdoches, and Shelby formed the northern boundary of Galveston.

1892
Right Reverend Nicholas Gallagher, D.D., succeeded to the title of Bishop of Galveston.
Right Reverend C.M. Dubuis was promoted to the archbishopric in partibus infidelium.

1907
Right Reverend Nicholas Gallagher celebrated his twenty-fifth anniversary as bishop of Galveston on April 30.

1918
The death of Bishop Nicholas Gallagher, D.D., on January 21.

1918
The Right Reverend Christopher Edward Byrne was consecrated the fourth bishop of Galveston on November 10.

1922
The solemn celebration of the Diamond Jubilee of the Diocese of Galveston and St. Mary's Cathedral.

While the 131-page book conveying the history of the Diocese of Galveston was compiled by the priests of the Seminary, one may wonder whether the actual writing was done by Fr. James Kirwin himself.

Guests for this week of remembrances included two archbishops and eight bishops. Several pontifical Masses were on the agenda. The historical tableau was presented at the end of the week.

It must have taken an extraordinary amount of research and many painstaking hours to put these tableaux together, making it a delightful gathering for the guests. Reverend Marius S. Chataignon supervised this work. Within the presentation, he was assisted by Adoph D. Dolson, Eugene Coughlin, and Charles K. Lalor.

Historical Tableaux

Tableau I: "Quivira Was Always Just Beyond," 1541

Tableau II: Death of Lasalle, 1687 A.D.

Tableau III: Founding of San Francisco de los Tejas, 1690 A.D.
Tableau IV: Brazos de Dios, 1716 A.D.

Tableau V: San Antonio De Valero, 1718 Avr. J.-C.
The Alamo, 1722 A.D.

Tableau VI: La Purissima Concepcion

Tableau VII: San Jacinto Battlefield, 1836

Tableau VIII: Father Timon, C.M., coming to address the Congress of the Republic of Texas,
Houston, January 1839. Present site of Rice Hotel

Tableau IX: Bishop Odin

Tableau X: Battle of Galveston, January 1, 1863

Tableau XI: Battle of Sabine Pass, 1863

Tableau XII: Bishop Claude Marie Dubuis

Tableau XIII: Bishop Gallagher

Tableau XIV: The Morning after the Storm, 1900

Tableau XV: The Cathedral

"Gather Up the Fragments that Remain
Lest They Be Lost."
—John. VI. 12.

DIAMOND JUBILEE

1847 -- 1922

OF

THE DIOCESE OF GALVESTON

AND

ST. MARY'S CATHEDRAL

COMPILED BY

THE PRIESTS OF THE SEMINARY

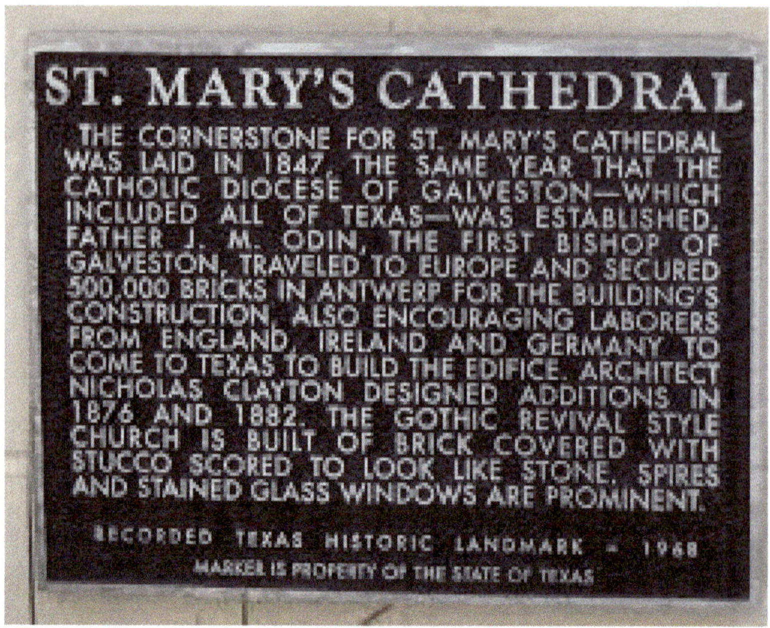

[37] The historical marker is found on the left side of the entrance to the Cathedral.

Patriotism: Victory after World War I

It is well known that Fr. Kirwin was a great patriot, having served as Chaplain whenever possible.

When victory was declared after World War I, Fr. Kirwin delivered a patriotic sermon on November 21, 1918. This was shortly after Armistice Day, which was November 11, 1918. A summary follows, illustrating the strength of his vigor in reference to what had passed and what he perceived as lying ahead.

---

[37]The historical marker is found on the left side of the entrance to the Cathedral. Historical Marker Database.

Fr. Kirwin, in a special way, referenced the American soldiers during the War. He mentioned the fighting at Chatigny, the first major American battle and offensive, fought May 28, 1918, and the victorious march of the American soldiers to the Rhine. The German Emperor was interned in Holland, and an armistice was signed in the Compiegne Forest on November 11, 1918. Fr. Kirwin perceived the Armistice as a "glorious and lasting peace." [38] We know that history conveys that the Treaty of Versailles, signed the following year on June 28, 1919, contained a war guilt clause against Germany and the other Central Powers. In addition, Germany's heavy debt payments became a major factor in the outbreak of the Second World War.

Unfortunately, the French experienced casualties of 4,500,000, the British, 2,000,000. American losses were 90,000. The total loss in lives was seven million. The cost was $250,000,000,000. The Americans, as Fr. Kirwin stated, were proud to fight for freedom and liberty. As he proclaimed, we are not here to boast but to give thanks. He brought forth the words of Abraham Lincoln: "Government of the people, by the people, for the people shall not perish from the earth."

Looking back at the action of the War, Fr. Kirwin recalled that the Germans had won the war several times. He described their intelligence service as perfect, that is, perfect behind their own lines, but in the affairs of the Allies, a failure. During the Battle of the Marne, or rather the Miracle of the Marne, there was an opening of

---

[38] Fr. James Kirwin, "Victory after World War I," *Memoirs of Monsignor J.M. Kirwin,* George T. Elmendorf, Compiler, n.p.

approximately twelve miles, but the Germans did not see it. (September 6-12 1914) The French pushed the Germans back 40-50 miles and saved the city of Paris. Again, there was an opening at Ypres to the channel ports. Yet, the Germans did not see it. Then the British army left an opening of approximately twelve miles directly to Amiens. German intelligence failed again.

Fr. Kirwin then went on to convey the story of Kemmel Hill. The French troops, who fought so hard in this battle, were a lost brigade; therefore, without orders. They threw a "little French cement into the wavering line," [39] preventing the taking of the channel ports. Fr. Kirwin stated that we do see God's Providence in the Lost Brigade that saved the Channel Ports. Despite the great ability of Marshal Foch, certainly God's Providence had a hand in winning this war.

Fr. Kirwin paid great respect to Georges Guynemer, the Frenchman who had 54 victories at the time of his death. He was a daily communicant and thanked God every time he came down to the altar.

He further gave thanks to those who built Annapolis and West Point, who built an army of four million men at that time.

Fr. Kirwin expressed the desire that all should be thankful for the benefit of peace. Men will be coming home to enter into peaceful occupations. In the meantime, American troops occupied Strasbourg and Metz. Those who served at home did their share in the war effort. There is a gratefulness extended to all.

In turning to the parable of the leaven, we are reminded how the baker mixes the dough. The chemist states that the dough contains

---

[39] Ibid.

dead cells. "We can only penetrate when we are good citizens. Unless we do our full duty, we are dead cells." [40]

"Look out on the sunlit sea; look up at our starry flag floating in glory for our soldiers on the Rhine, and with grateful hearts give thanks unto God for all His blessings." [41]

[42] World War I "Ring It Again" 2nd Liberty Loan Poster

---

[40] Ibid.

[41] Ibid.

[42] "World War I 'Ring It Again' 2nd Liberty Loan Poster," Courtesy of the Library of Congress.

Fr. Kirwin paid great attention to the liturgical cycle as he preached every Sunday at Mass and more frequently at St. Mary's Seminary.

His mantra for the following sermon is found in the line that the Church is a spiritual, not a social, agent. During the liturgical cycle at that time, it was the fourth Sunday after Easter.

The homilist drew from the letter of James the phrase: "Be quick to hear and slow to speak and slow to anger" (James 1:19). This runs contrary to our everyday inclinations. We tend to refuse to listen. We are inclined to gossip. We become angry at little things. The line from the letter of James is of tremendous benefit if we would only heed it.

According to the gospel of John, the Church is not a social agent, but as already stated, a spiritual agent. The work of the Holy Spirit is "to convince the world of sin, of justice and of judgment, and teach all truth. Therein is the entire work of Christ's Church" (John 16:8). It is this Church which has the obligation to keep the judgment of the eternal years before us, that is, all would have lived their life in vain "if they gain the whole world and lost their immortal souls" (Mark 8:36).

The promise of our Master does not change. In fact, it is our hope. It is this message that is meant to change the minds and hearts of men so that we take the message in its fullness and conform our actions to its saving principles.

Yet, the message of St. Paul may seem "to catch the momentary phases of the world and intensely grip them."[43] For St. Paul states, "Our wrestling is not against flesh and blood, but against principalities and powers, against the rulers of the world of darkness, against the spirit of wickedness in high places." (Eph 6:12). So, we are urged to pray for our President that he may know God's light and strength. We are called to be on duty, in that sense. We all have visions and ways of justice we would like to see done. Yet, it is difficult not to hear the call from the Gospel, "Lord, come down before my son dies" (John 4:49). That wish, that prayer, has been on the lips of countless mothers and fathers. We pray that the wish of the psalmist be realized, "Peace and justice have kissed" (Psalm 85:11).

The cry of the Good Samaritan calls one to exercise mercy toward his fellow man. That call can be heard in hospitals, orphanages, and homes for the elderly. The "ministry of pain is not of yesterday. Science has given it direction and security, but science cannot keep the hearts throbbing and the recruits coming. It is only the appeal of humanity and religion that bends the strong to serve the weak."[44]

Fr. Kirwin reminded his listeners that the parable of the Good Samaritan (Lk 10: 29-37) has a spiritual as well as a physical message. He called upon the great Greek Church Father, St. John Chrysostom (347-407), who was known as a renowned orator, the golden tongue, and a learned Church Father. Within that parable, Chrysostom interpreted the man as Adam, who fell into sin and was robbed of virtue and grace. The priest and the Levite did not help him, but the

---

[43] Fr. James Kirwin, "The Good Samaritan," *Memoirs of Monsignor J.M. Kirwin*, George T. Elmendorf, Compiler, n.p.

[44] Ibid.

good Samaritan, whom he saw as Jesus Christ, picked him up and put him in the inn of the Church. He demanded from the innkeeper that he be nourished, stating that when He returned to him, he would reward those who took care of the man. He poured oil and wine into the man's wounds and fed him. The sacraments of Penance and Eucharist were very much within the mind of St. John Chrysostom. He called upon those listening that we have the obligation to care for the wounded, in body and soul.

We know that St. John Chrysostom died in exile, as he spoke courageously against the immorality of the royal court in Constantinople. Chrysostom chose to remain firm in his advocacy of a moral life. Amazingly, he would not hold anger against those in authority who chastised him grievously. He himself was a great Samaritan, like that of the Christ he depicted in the parable.

Fr. Kirwin closed his sermon: "May something of the tender pity, the loving service, the absence of selfishness that illuminates the good Samaritan find its reflection in our individual and social lives." [45]

---

[45] Ibid.

[46] The Good Samaritan

Self-Denial – Looking at the Essence of Religion

Not long before World War I ended (January 13, 1918), Fr. Kirwin preached on the virtue of self-denial, emphasizing that it is a cardinal element in the life of every Christian. He described self-denial as of the very essence of religion. We have been "trained" to

[46] "The Good Samaritan," *The Central Minnesota Catholic.*

sacrifice in the cause of Christ, additionally, as he stated, in the cause of the country. He described it as "holy, pleasing to God." [47]

The Church, in its care of souls, warns against reading materials that are bad for the soul, that are heretical or suggestive. The unity of the Church demands supervision.

In noting the Catholic population of the country, the celebrant stated that it was one-sixth of the entire population. Within the local army camps, then, Camps Logan and MacArthur, one-third of those camps were Catholic. That, as he stated, was gratifying. He presumed that Catholics were as generous across the country. Some once thought that parochial school education would be a hindrance to the unification of our country. Rather, it has served the country well. In that sense, the Church is grateful.

The Gospel passage, "He went down to Nazareth and was subject to them" (LK 2:51), provides the beautiful example of obedience to parental authority. Would it not follow that this model provides children with the admiration to follow? That, in turn, could enable them to "advance in wisdom and age and grace before God and men."(LK 2:52)

Fr. Kirwin noted the example of the Good Shepherd as drawn from the Gospel: "Other sheep I have that are not of this fold, them also I must bring, and there shall be one fold and one shepherd" (John 10:16). Certainly, a thousand examples have been brought forth of the Good Shepherd. It brings to mind the Good Shepherd Sisters who work so industriously with women who need a second

---

[47] Fr. James Kirwin, "Self-Denial, Looking at the Essence of Religion," *Memoirs of Monsignor J.M. Kirwin* George T. Elmendorf, Compiler, n.p.

chance to start their lives anew. The Sisters were called forth to serve in the Galveston diocese by Bishop Nicholas Gallagher. Referring to the passage from the gospels, "The Good Shepherd lays down His life for His sheep" (John 10:11), Fr. Kirwin noted that there is a marble slab at the entrance to St. Mary's Cathedral commemorating the five priests who lie buried there. They did not allow pestilence or other obstacles to get in the way of serving the Good Shepherd. Fr. Kirwin emphasized that no man comes back from the front who does not admire the spiritual and military leadership of the French clergy.

Four hundred Americans were out on the high seas, ready to make the complete sacrifice. Fr. Kirwin asked parents if they ever bring forth the image of the Good Shepherd to their children. The command to pray for the unity of the Church rests as much upon those in the pew as it does upon the clergy.

Christ prayed for the unity of the Church in the Garden of Gethsemane. "That they may all be one as You, Father, are in Me and I in Thee" (John 17:21). Today, as Fr. Kirwin states, Christ cries out, "One fold and one shepherd" (John 10:16). We are all called to pray for the unity of Christ's Church.

The men at war will come back with marvelous stories of human sacrifice. The celebrant trusted that we would be able to meet their high ideals in the cause of this country and turn it into spiritual gifts for each other. Faith must not only be professed. It must be shown in works, that is, in deeds. We are called to give ourselves as generously as the soldiers did in the service of their country in the service of "the way, the truth, and the life" (John 14:6). [48]

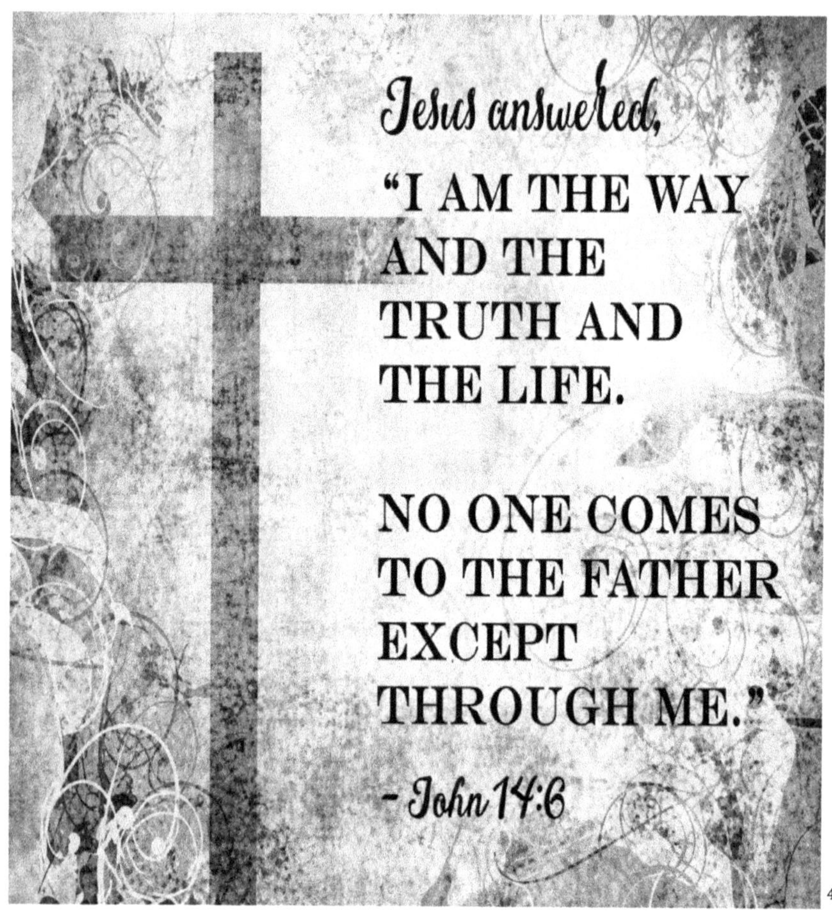

[49]

[48] Ibid.

[49] "I am the Way, the truth, and the life (Jn14:6)," Bibleinspirations.org.

Parable of the Mustard Seed

The parable of the mustard seed is meant to convey that we should stand in awe that Christianity first survived and then grew. Christ chose the mustard seed, the smallest of all seeds, to convey the unlikelihood of its growth. Further, one would not have assumed that the mustard seed could grow into a tree in maturity. "The kingdom of heaven is like a mustard seed that a person took and sowed in a field. It is the smallest of all the seeds, yet when full-grown, it is the largest of plants. It becomes a large bush, and the birds of the sky come and dwell in its branches" (Mt 13:31-32).

Initially, it seemed most unlikely that Christianity could survive. After all, its Founder was born to very unassuming parents. He was crucified, the most difficult of deaths, as a criminal. Unfortunately, the Romans utilized this very difficult form of death, which they obtained from the Persians. Those whom Christ asked to follow Him were rude Hebrew peasants whom He had gathered around the lakesides and hillsides of Galilee. What Christ taught was difficult to understand and hard to follow. These teachings ran counter to the culture of Greece and the power of the Roman Empire. Yet despite the penalties of persecution and death, the message traveled to Athens, then the center of the world's culture, and to Rome, the center of the world's power. From these points, the religion triumphed. It was thought that the influence of a Roman council would have ended the movement, if one wishes to call it that. Yet, within three centuries this cross of Christianity was found on the banners of Constantine, "In this sign Thou shall conquer." The hand of God was there. The Lord had spoken, and thousands had followed.

As Fr. Kirwin stated, one cannot stop at the intellectual contemplation of the growth of the teachings of Christ's doctrine within the world. Those nations of the world that have accepted it can find rest and security in the tree's branches. There is yet another application. What growth has taken place within ourselves? Fr. Kirwin referred to the same seed of divine truth, justice, purity, and sobriety that has been planted in our own souls. The obligation rests within ourselves to act upon it, so that others may see the beauty of our faith and the security of the doctrine.

Yet, Christ conveyed another parable, "The kingdom of heaven is like yeast that a woman took and mixed with three measures of wheat flour until the whole batch was leavened" (Mt 13:33). Christ's doctrines have leavened or permeated the world. In the chemical or fermenting process, each cell must carry on what it receives, or an additional burden is placed on the original mass and surrounding cells. "Where cells fail to assimilate their portion, a space results." [50] This can certainly be likened to the Christian life. The Catholic who resists God's grace and therefore fails to observe truth, justice, purity, and sobriety, becomes that void. Others, therefore, must carry the beauty and security of her teachings.

Fr. Kirwin asked what influence we have had upon those who have come into contact with us. Referring to St. Paul's First Letter to the Thessalonians, he states, "For from you the word of the Lord has

---

[50]Fr. James Kirwin, "The Parable of the Mustard Seed," *Memoirs of Monsignor J.M. Kirwin,* George T. Elmendorf, Compiler, n.p.

sounded forth not only in Macedonia and in Achaia, but in every place your faith in God has gone forth, so that we have no need to say anything" (1 Thes 1:8). What is so terribly important is the example the Christian community has set. Fr. Kirwin stated, "The divine leaven has not lost its power. Spiritually, we do not carry on."[51] For we are wanting in charity. We are critical of others and self-centered. "We lack that high sense of justice that should characterize a Christian, and the outside world believes our religion is but a Sunday suit."[52]

We fail to tell the truth for the sake of material gain. "When God and country together call, we are hesitant and prefer our own physical comfort to our neighbor's needs."[53] A renewal of this leavening process must begin with ourselves. He urges us not to be concerned about our neighbor's failure to carry on. Rather, we are called to be mindful of the faith, labor, charity, and the enduring hope we have in our Lord Jesus Christ.[54]

Hearers and Doers of the Word

The Scriptures that Fr. Kirwin was drawn to for a particular Sunday have much to do with women and acting on the Word.

The names of two women, Erodia and Syntyche, were mentioned, individuals who are uncommon to us but very important to St. Paul in writing to the people of Philippi. Much was

---

[51] Ibid.

[52] Ibid.

[53] Ibid.

[54] Ibid.

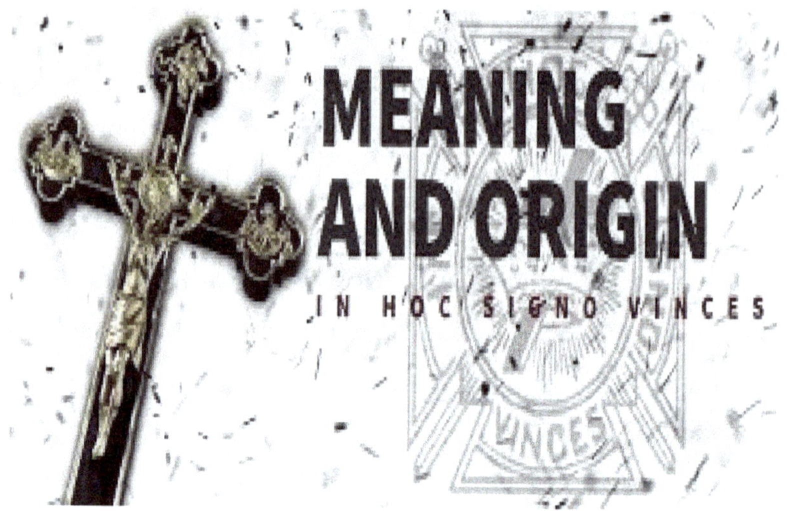

[55] In this sign thou shalt conquer.
Christ commanded Constantine in a vision the night before battle to use the cross on his labarum to conquer in battle, which he did.

revealed about the status of women. These two women were disagreeing about some issue that was terribly important to them. It is well to note that this dispute became public and between two women. Paul begs the women to resolve their disagreement, but he asks the other Christians in the community to assist them. Paul also mentions that these two women have struggled alongside him in spreading the Gospel, as have other co-workers. Paul does not wish a disagreement to be a distraction in the ministry (Phil 4:2-3).

The second passage Fr. Kirwin addressed comes from Luke, who does give special attention to women. The emphasis was cast on a lived faith. A woman who had been suffering from a hemorrhage knew that if she just touched Jesus, she would be healed. Thus Jesus

[55] Templar cross.com.

responded, "Someone has touched me; for I know that power has gone out from me." (LK 8:46) The woman, realizing that she must respond, came forth trembling. When she fell before Him, she explained that she was healed instantly. Jesus immediately responded, "Daughter, your faith has saved you; go in peace." (Lk 8:47-48)

In a certain sense, acting on the Word is most apparent in these two readings. It is essential, in the first reading, that the two women resolve their differences so that St. Paul's ministry might continue. It became a public matter in such a way that anyone who could offer a solution could do so. While this might call the two women to humility in the exposure of their disagreement, all virtue had to be put into practice to further the building of the Church.

The letter of St. James is filled with such practical advice. In that sense, it is often quoted within the liturgy. However, James is not often quoted among many of our Protestant brethren. Some question its authenticity, and others do not wish to give attention to the sacrament of the Anointing of the Sick.

Thus, we come to the Eucharist that we might be strengthened in our application of the Word of God. We wish first to see our faults and then find means to correct them. However, as we become so involved in our daily occupations, we fail to live up to our inspirations. As St. James says, "For if anyone is a hearer of the word and not a doer, he is like a man who looks at his own face in a mirror. He sees himself, then goes off and promptly forgets what he looked like" (James 1:23-24). Unfortunately, in the world we live in, our cohorts do not normally see great spiritual conversions evident in our actions. Therefore, it could be said by the onlooker, "This man's religion is vain." [56]

Fr. Kirwin saw St. James with a plan of action: "Religion that is pure and undefiled before God and the Father is this: to look after orphans and widows in their affliction and to keep oneself unstained by the world" (James 1:27). It is difficult to keep oneself unstained by the world. Yet that is what we strive for. The celebrant mentioned that we are hesitant to express our religious convictions before the world, whether that be in wearing a scapular or using a rosary. Do we make the sign of the cross when we pass before a Catholic Church? We must strive to carry the cause of Christ to its heights and "win the world's obedience to His mandates" so that we also might be doers of His Word. [57]

Hearers of the Word vs. Doers of the Word

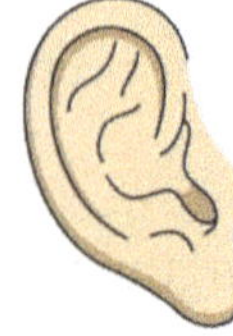

- Hearers
  - Deceive themselves
  - Forget who they are
  - Do not persevere
  - And so they do not do, that is, live out the life of faith

- Doers
  - Are not deceiving themselves
  - Remember who they are
  - Persevere
  - And so they do, that is, live out the life of faith

[58] Catholic Sunday Scripture

---

[56]Fr. James Kirwin, "Hearers and Doers of the Word," *Memoirs of Monsignor J.M. Kirwin* George T. Elmendorf, Compiler, n.p.

[57] Ibid.

[58] "Hearers of the Word vs Doers of the Video," *Catholic Sunday Scripture*. Linkedin.com.

Strength Gained through Prayer

The Church will always face opposition in this world. Therefore, the faithful follower can expect trial and persecution. The faithful are called to practice prudence and naturally be prayerful individuals. Prayer is the ordinary food of the soul. If our life is without prayer, we cannot expect to conquer our passions. Know likewise, there are temptations out there from the world, the flesh, and the devil.

St. Peter tells the faithful to be prudent and watchful in prayer. How does Fr. Kirwin describe prayer? Simply, it is the speaking of the individual with his Creator. At times, it involves the weak pleading for God's protection. It is also the song of praise for the grateful person. Neglect in prayer is as harmful to the soul as a lack of nourishment is to the body.

Beyond the awareness of the great strength through prayer, St. Peter secondly suggests the practice of charity. We are called to "a mutual constant charity" among ourselves, for as St. Peter iterates, "charity covers a multitude of sins" (1 Peter 4:8). According to Fr. Kirwin, St. Peter was referring to the "kindly thought." He desired that charity to be constant. Fr. Kirwin described it as "the continued flow of tender love toward our neighbor." [59] It needs to be mutual. The man who violates it by revealing his neighbor's faults, by conveying what he believes his motives are, or by criticizing his conduct, is sure to have his own defects revealed. So, when it is said

Fr. James Kirwin, "Strength Gained through Prayer," *Memoirs of Monsignor J.M. Kirwin,* George T. Elmendorf, Compiler, n.p.[59]

that charity covers a multitude of sins, it is not only our neighbor's sins but also those of our own.

Fr. Kirwin refers to the Gospel, which reminds the listener that we are called to give testimony to Christ. That means more than a profession of faith. Rather, it is also the doing of the word. Trial and persecution need to be expected. The generous response of the Church and its members when the country is in need is meant to silence slander and bigotry that might otherwise be heard. As Fr. Kirwin so aptly uttered, bigotry was forced to stand at attention.

We are each tried by fire with the worthwhile matters. Opposition will only strengthen one's resolve and firm one's purpose to do what was originally focused on. [60] So, when opposition develops and false motives are assigned, the words of Christ are so very apt: "You may remember that I told you of them" (John 15:18).

God will not Let You Be Tried Beyond Your Strength.

There is a stark phrase coming from St. Paul's letter to the Romans. Fr. Kirwin has chosen to emphasize it, and with good reason. That phrase, "The wages of sin are death" (Rom 6:23), is rather stark in itself. It holds its own truth, for sin separates us from God. It can lead to spiritual death if we allow that to happen. We do not have to allow that to happen, however. The second part of that statement is life-giving, for as it says, "the gift of God is eternal life in Christ Jesus our Lord" (Rom 6:23). Thus, the gift of God's grace is what is life-giving. We only need to say yes to that. Sin certainly

[60] Ibid.

has its own consequences, for it weakens us spiritually, in that we have created that distance from God. Hopefully, that is not for long, for we recognize our foolishness, correct our mistakes, and realize again the tremendous selfless love Christ has for us, even though we have allowed ourselves to be disillusioned by the things of this world. It is important to bear in mind that eternal life comes to us through the redemptive act of Jesus Christ, again, that totally selfless love in the midst of our sinful acts.

Paul is addressing the weakness of human nature. Specifically, he looks at the infirmity of the flesh. In the past, one's sins may have made one a slave to the flesh. It is possible to make that complete turn. This turn is seen in the expression "slaves to righteousness for sanctification" (Rom 6:19). Thus, when we become slaves of God, the end is eternal life.

St. Paul certainly does not mean that this transformation will take place immediately. Rather, we are called to educate for contingency. The Catholic Church, as Fr. Kirwin stated, is the world's oldest institution. She has been training men and women in chastity for centuries. We are called to discipline the soul and insist upon its responsibilities before God and the Church. Youth need to be trained in the ways of the commandments. They must come to know the strength found in prayer, mortification of the senses, and self-denial. The sacraments, further, are a great protection against the attractions of the world. The more frequently we receive them, the better off we are. When we do fail, and we will, we beg the good Lord for His mercy. We know that the Gospels are rich in conveying the examples of Christ's mercy. St. Paul does not hesitate to invoke these prayers of mercy for himself.

Recalling what he told the Corinthian community, "God is faithful and will not let you be tried beyond your strength" (1 Cor 10:13). Paul certainly recognized his own temptations and loved the Lord mightily enough to fight fiercely against them.

Moving on to the Gospels, specifically Matthew's Gospel, we encounter the phrase, "By their fruits you shall know them" (Mt 7:16). These words come directly from Christ Himself. Ultimately, it is how we lead our lives in conformity to the teachings of Christ that wins for us the approval of our neighbors. In that sense, society looks at the person of action and the life that he lives. Fr. Kirwin called upon the wisdom of St. Hilary of Poitiers, writing in the mid-fourth century, "It is not by what we say we are in words, but by what we prove ourselves to be in deeds, that the world shall judge our doctrine." So, in carrying that further, it is not the lives of saints, or the beauty of the liturgy, but simply again, the deeds that we live. [61]

[62]

[61] Ibid.

[62] "God Is Faithful," Pinterest.com.

Sacred Heart Church

Sacred Heart Parish enjoys a long history in Galveston. While its present structure has not had an enduring history, the presence of the Jesuits has been tied to Galveston for several decades.

The Michael Menard family gave the land on which the present Church stands. The Parish itself was established on June 21, 1884, by Bishop Nicholas Gallagher, the third bishop of Galveston. The first Mass was celebrated on July 15, 1884. Fr. John O'Connor began the parish, assisted by Fr. Slevin. In 1892, it was the largest Church in Texas. Sacred Heart Church was closely connected with St. Mary's University, which was located in Galveston at that time. Unfortunately, the 1900 storm devastated most of the original building. Only two stained glass windows, a statue of the Sacred Heart, the Mass bell, and the crucifix for the Church survived. These items remain within the Church today.

Nicholas Clayton designed the present building. The parish family made plans for rebuilding the Church. Bishop Gallagher gave generously toward the rebuilding of the Church from funds collected all over the United States. The cornerstone was laid on June 21, 1903. The Church was consecrated on January 17, 1904. Fr. D.J. Murphy was the pastor at the time of the construction. The building is known for its octagonal towers, flying buttresses, and a variety of arches. The dome is one hundred feet high, and the altar and communion rail are made of marble. [63] The building's design reflects varied styles: Moorish, Romanesque, Byzantine, and Gothic. [64]

The Pontifical Mass on June 20, 1909, was in commemoration of the 25th anniversary of Sacred Heart Church. As previously stated, the first Mass was celebrated on July 15, 1884. Fr. Kirwin specifically called to mind the sons of St. Ignatius of Loyola. As a youth, Ignatius was challenged to fight against the French king, Francis I, who was invading Navarre. Unfortunately, he was wounded in battle and taken prisoner by the French. He endured two painful operations, which left him limping for the remainder of his life. Upon getting back to his home, for the soldiers had to carry him one hundred miles on a stretcher, his recuperation was only aided by reading books entailing the Life of Christ and the lives of the saints. As a result of his conversion, he was moved to give up his military life to follow the imitation of the lives of the saints. Some of his spiritual experiences are captured in his *Spiritual Exercises.* Ignatius hung up his arms at the shrine of the Blessed Mother at Montserrat. He pledged himself to the service of Christ and moved on to Manresa, taking on the image of a pilgrim. Much of his *Exercises* were composed at Manresa. He then went on to Rome and took a pilgrimage to Jerusalem. He traveled through Barcelona, Alcala, and Salamanca and finally enrolled at the University of Paris. There, at a subterranean chapel at the Abbey of Montmartre, Peter Faber, Francis Xavier, Diego Lainez, Alfonso Salmeron, Nicolas Bobadilla, and Rodriguez of Azevedo made vows of poverty and chastity. They

---

[63] Giles, *Changing Times*, 102-103.

[64] Christina Strommen Stevens, "The Historical Sacred Heart Church in Galveston, Texas. A True Beauty of Our Time."

bound themselves to the service of the Church and the conversion of infidels. This simple ceremony had a tremendous effect on Catholic education in the service of the Church. Six years later, in 1540, Pope Paul III gave them solemn approval. They became the "strongest battalion" within the Catholic Church's spiritual army. They have served the Church well for the past four centuries. Fr. Kirwin described them as "the Pope's own." This band, known as the Company of Jesus, adopted an uncompromising orthodoxy and an intense Catholic spirit. Their banner, "Ad Majorem Dei Gloriam," "For the Greater Glory of God," has flown since. They have established institutions of learning at the high school and collegiate levels worldwide. Further, they have become "an object of terror" in the minds of many Protestants. Their own attempts at conveying the teachings of truth and justice have not always been met with great serenity within the Church. "Blessed are you when men shall revile and persecute you and say all manner of evil against you falsely for my sake, for your reward is very great in heaven" (Mt 5:11-12).

In his sermon, Fr. Kirwin enumerated some of the early Jesuits' accomplishments. He singled out Diego Lainez and Alfonso Salmeron for their contributions to the Council of Trent, which was held in Trent from 1545 to 1563 in separate sessions. The purpose of the Council was to reaffirm the teachings of the Church after the confusion of the Protestant Reformation. He mentioned Francis Borgia, who gave up a royal life at the Spanish court after his wife, who was the queen, died. He himself had undergone a conversion experience which led to his entry into the Society. Francis Xavier was extolled for his mission work in the Far East. Fr. Kirwin recognized him as the heroic Alexander of souls. In his travels to the Far East, he was known for his chanting, "In te Domini speravi." Stanislaus Kostka and Aloysius Gonzaga were recognized as models for youth. They each died quite young. There is so much that could be written and said about many other giants within the Society of Jesus. This would include Peter Canisius, Robert Bellarmine, Leonardus Lessius, Francisco Suarez, Franciscus Toletus, and Cornelius de Lapide. They were intellectual giants in their day who became known in varied cities in Europe, from Munich to Cologne, to Treves, to Innsbruck, and other Jesuit foundations. They were "checking the progress of religious revolution" and sending missionaries to parts of the world that had never heard of Christ.

François René Chateaubriand burst with a marvelous admiration for the Jesuits in their missionary extension.

Referring to the seventy-two volumes of the *Jesuit Relations*, the stories of those missionaries in what was referred to at the time as New France are so found, whether it be a Jacquette Marquette, Isaac Jogues, John de Brebeuf, or Pierre Lallemant. Chateaubriand provided his description of the "Reduction" or "Christian Commonwealth" of Paraguay.

The suppression soon followed. Lorenzo Ricci was asked to change the course and alter the purpose of the society, but he refused: "Sint ut sint, aut non sint." Let them remain or let them cease to be." Seventy-five thousand Jesuits were subject to unjust humiliation. They made no complaint when "Dominus et Redemptor" was issued. Fortunately, they came back stronger, as Francis Bacon described the Jesuit Order as a perfect invention. 2014 celebrated the 200th anniversary of the Restoration.

Fifty years after the time that Fr. Kirwin commemorated the anniversary of Sacred Heart Church, the Oblates of Mary, under the guidance of Fr. Parisot, established St. Mary's University. Bishop Odin requested this. The Society for the Propagation of the Faith in France, in addition to the Catholic planters of Louisiana, provided the means for this to come about. For thirty years, this institution had success, then almost failed. The Christian Brothers, in addition to the Fathers of the Holy Cross, labored in this Institution.

Diocesan priests and lay teachers struggled to keep the Institution alive in later years. Finally, Bishop Gallagher asked the Jesuits to cast their mantle of science and religion. Thus, for a quarter-century, it had been under Jesuit control. The people of Galveston built a beautiful Sacred Heart Church, but, unfortunately, it was washed away by the storm of 1900. The memory of the old Sacred Heart Church remains. When the Bishop proclaimed that "Galveston needs you," the population of Galveston got busy again. A roll call of all those who helped would require another quarter of a century. Yet, we pay a special debt of gratitude to all those who built this magnificent Church, to the Jesuits and clergy of the diocese, and, readily, the Bishop, without whom none of it would have been possible. [65]

---

[65] Fr. James Kirwin," Sacred Heart Church," *Memoirs of Monsignor J.M. Kirwin,* George T. Elmendorf, Compiler, n.p.

[66] Sacred Heart Church, Galveston

[67] Sacred Heart Church, Galveston

---

[66] Sacred Heart Church, Galveston, Holyfamilygb.com.
[67] Sacred Heart Church, Galveston, Holyfamilygb.com.

[68] Jesuit Schools Logo

[69] Patron Saints of the Military

---

[68] Jesuitinstitute.org.

[69] Catholictradition.org.

70

Their wealth remains in their families,
their heritage with their descendants; Ireland's Patron Saint
Through God's covenant with them, their family endures,
their posterity for their sake.
And for all time their progeny will endure,
their glory will never be blotted out;
Their bodies are peacefully laid away,
But their name lives on and on.
At gatherings, their wisdom is retold,
and the assembly proclaims their praise.
(Ecclesiasticus 44: 11-15)

Fr. Kirwin chose to honor St. Patrick by conveying a legend of the saint. Patrick often described himself as "an unworthy and ignorant and sinful man." [71]After toiling over sixty years, for he had

---

[70] Catholic News Agency.

[71] Patrick of Armagh, *Confessions of St. Patrick,* trans. John Skinner, in *Confessions of St Patrick and Letter to Coroticus* (Mass Market Paperbacks, 1998), 1.

traveled the island throughout its four kingdoms from one end to the other, Patrick, the Apostle, the Saint, was wearied with the labors of Christ. His message of Catholic dogmas and Christian virtues was so embedded in the hearts of his hearers that it has echoed for fifteen centuries pure and undefiled in the blood of Irish children.

He could hear the voices of noble men and virginal daughters chanting the praises of Jesus Christ. He had seen the Druids vanquished and the first line of Irish priests, brought forth by himself, engaging in a battle for souls. He could see his Christian children moving in a pilgrim procession due to those sixty years of toil. Yet he looked back and believed he had done little for the cause of Christ. His children could trace the three score years from the time he landed at the mouth of the Dea in Wicklow until his earthly labors were complete. Patrick, an intense lover of souls, proceeded under the guidance of an angelic visitor to Down's sacred soil to die. So his body was deposited in Down's hallowed earth, and his soul passed on to its eternal reward.

At the beginning of his missionary journey, the Church was full of vitality, battling for souls. She was meeting heretics such as Nestorius in the east, Pelagius in the west, and the Manichees in Africa. It was the time of Augustine, Germain of Paris, Vincent of Lerins, John Chrysostom, Gregory of Nyssa, Jerome, Basil the Great, Ambrose of Milan, and Athanasius. Yet none of them had a wider influence on his anniversary than Patrick, save St. Peter himself. Eloquent tongues told the stories of his earthly pilgrimage. Hearts charged with love and faith could convey the circumstances of his death. Legend conveys that immediately before his death, his angelic guide informed him that his spirit was about to be dissolved and be with Christ. He thus prayed on bended knee, reflecting on the "dim and distant future." He saw the destiny of Innisfail (Ireland). Then he prayed for the constancy, the fidelity of the chosen people of the new law. He prayed as a reward for his personal labors, "May my Lord grant that I may never lose the people which He has acquired in the ends of the earth." He asked for the unusual privilege of judging the Irish people at the end of the world. His request was refused, which only increased his zeal. The earnestness of his desire won from God the extraordinary favor, and then his soul was taken to the courts of heaven. Has that prayer of Patrick been answered, and who shall come before him on judgment day?

According to this legend, his prayer was answered. The response rings true down the centuries. The children of Patrick's missionaries continue to spread the faith. The first faint strains were caught up by Secundinus to Benignus, by Columba and Columbanus, by Brigid and Brendan. As the legend states, the faith floats away from Lindisfarne to Iceland and Tarentum. It is heard on the banks of the Rhine. It breaks against the crags of the Alps. It re-echoes within the gates of Rome. Patrick enumerated the children of the faith: the patron of Austria, 150 canonized saints of Germany, 450 in France, 44 in England, 13 in Italy, 8 in Norway, and Sweden. All the children of Patrick, devoted followers, brought the gospel to Switzerland and Scotland and gave testimony to this truth.

Referring to the destiny of Innisfail, that is, Ireland, although Erin is actually a more familiar name, the Irish church has become the prolific mother of saints. This can be seen especially from the fifth through the ninth centuries. The continent was plunged into darkness as the rude barbarians, unfortunately, devastated the seats of learning and the houses of prayer. The Emerald Isle is shown on the Western sea with its learning in science, literature, and, of course, religion. These must be seen as the time of her pride and joy. At that time, she held intellectual supremacy in the world, and her sons were the apostles of Europe, the founders of schools, and the teachers of doctors. She was seen as the "Isle of Saints and Doctors." It was the time of glory for the schools of Armagh and Lismore. Glendalough, founded in the sixth century by St. Kevin, was regarded as the "luminary of the western world" for the prayer and praise that arose from it. St. Fionan founded Muckross in the sixth century. It was called the "rock of music" because of the mysterious sounds that came forth. Due to its violent history, largely at the hands of its enemies in Great Britain, it had to be rebuilt and repaired several times. Holy Cross Abbey is remembered for having a relic of the True Cross. Whereas many tongues could be heard on the streets outside, within the abbey, at matins and vespers, the chanting of the universal language of the Church, Latin, echoed. The hills housed the hermitages of anchorites. The valleys possessed the footsteps of saints. The tower watches over the graves of God's people buried at this site. The number of churches around cannot be counted. The monasteries and convents were the homes of the pious and the sites that took in the poor.

Fr. Kirwin stated that the people have been living in the past. They must not forget the wrongs which have been done to Ireland or the woes which the Emerald Isle experienced, the dismantled churches and crumbling oratories. She became the prolific mother of saints. With the current crises in the world, Patrick's prayer was being put to the test. As Fr. Kirwin stated, persecution and suffering are the tests of faith in nations and individuals. One can certainly look at those areas in the world that experienced that suffering. The Moors, unfortunately, destroyed Christianity in the East. The Saracens brought much damage to the Alexandria of Mark the Evangelist. Carthage had been catechized by Cyprian and Hippo by Augustine. All experienced Christian devastation. The Danes certainly invaded Ireland, but left it as Catholic as ever. Those going to the Holy Land could recall in history how Christians left these holy sites. Sword, famine, broken walls, and slaughtered priests all had made it very difficult for Christianity to endure.

The Irish fought for their homeland from the time the Normans landed in 1169 until Henry VIII took on the title of King of Ireland in 1549. Were the Irish people willing to stand by the ancient faith? As Fr. Kirwin stated, the entire strength of earth's mightiest people was put forth against her. They were willing to stand as one man and pray that Patrick would help defend them. As brought forth by Fr. Kirwin, persecution could not reach the soul. The storm, however, was not a passing one, for the persecution of the Irish people went on for decades.

The faithful Irish priest helped the Irish populace along, casting from their lips any mention of heresy. Many Irish sailed from their shores never to return. The Irish priest followed. They went beyond their own shores for bread. All their thoughts centered around their faith. When a mother heard of the death of a son on a distant shore, her first thought was, did he die as a Catholic should, confessing his sins, with his trust in God, strengthened by reception of the sacraments? Yet, the Irish took with them to foreign lands a strong faith and with that faith, a courage to persevere in it. It was "the faith of our fathers." The Irish priest was the most important factor in the propagation of the faith. He kept alive the flame of faith and the love of freedom. He was rewarded with a heart-warming attachment and profound reverence.

These immigrants to foreign lands kept alive a great love of the solitary Island of Ireland. The ballad "Soggarth Aroon" expresses that great love of the Irish for their priests. Within the work, an old woman is seen dying in a strange land. She anxiously brings forth the question:

> When my body lies cold in the land of the stranger,
> Will my soul pass through Ireland on its way to God?"

The Irish immigrants brought none of the world's goods from beyond the sea, but they carried in their hearts " the priceless legacy of the Catholic faith and a childlike trust in God." [72] They further retained the "chastity, the unbroken courage, the cheerful temper, and generous love" [73] for which they were known at home. Thus, the prayer of Patrick withstood the test. Within the next life, the children of Patrick march before the good Lord with the canonized saints.

Yet, not all heard praises coming from the lips of the good Lord. Some cried out, "I have lost the priceless jewel of faith. I have sold the precious legacy of my forefathers for the world's vain joys and

---

[72]Fr. James Kirwin, "Ireland's Patron Saint," *Memoirs of Monsignor J.M. Kirwin* George T. Elmendorf, Compiler, n.p.

[73] Ibid.

fleeting hopes. I have forgotten God in strange lands." God grant that those who stand before the Lord pleading shall be few. [74]

[75]

My Grace Is Sufficient for You

In noting the parable of the Pharisee and the Publican, Fr. Kirwin drew on St. Augustine, for, as he stated, the Pharisee did not wish to ask God for anything. Rather, he wished to praise himself. Continuing in that spirit, he was proud, self-centered, and self-contained.

The publican asked God for mercy for his sins. Christ tells us that his prayer pierced the clouds and drew from God the forgiveness he asked for, and, further, he knew the fullness of grace. 'This man went down to his house justified (Lk 18:9-14).

Both character types exist today. Hopefully, like the publican, we ask God in humility for forgiveness for our sins. Fr. Kirwin referred

---

[74] Ibid.

[75] Who was St. Patrick? Celebration Ireland Catholic History.

to the leaders of the country who, in humility, urged the people to acknowledge their sins and pray for protection for the men at war. Who would have thought the throwing of a bomb in the streets of Sarajevo would enkindle a world war? How could one measure the evils the war has brought about? Yet, there were many other causes of the conflict. Who would have thought the United States would become involved? The celebrant, in humility and with contrite hearts, urged the members of the Congregation to continue their work in the world. He urged a remembrance of the scripture passage, "Everyone who exalts himself shall be humbled, and he that humbled himself shall be exalted" (Mt 23:12).

In referring to the Epistle and Gospel, Fr. Kirwin drew upon two moral suggestions from them, the infamous phrase, "The wages of sin are death." The Catholic Church, the world's oldest institution, has trained men and women to live lives of complete chastity for centuries. We must discipline our souls to purity and insist upon that responsibility in the sight of God. Many are free from physical defilement, but their souls are rotten. The commandments tell us Thou shalt not and then Thou shalt not covet. We are trained through self-denial and the mortification of the senses in our youth. The sacraments are a "trench" of protection against the attacks of the world. When we do fail, we ask the good Lord to have mercy on us. In its entirety, that passage from Romans reads, "For the wages of sin are death, but the gift of God is eternal life in Christ Jesus our Lord" (Rom 6:23).

St. Paul reminded his flock that we are not tempted beyond that which we are able. In other words, God's grace is sufficient for us. Again, the passage in its entirety, "My grace is sufficient for you, for power is made perfect in weakness. I will rather boast most gladly of my weaknesses so that the power of Christ may dwell within me" (2 Cor 12:9).

The second moral suggestion is drawn from the familiar scripture passage, "By their fruits you shall know them" (Mt 7:20). Fr. Kirwin then called upon Hilary of Poitiers, the fourth century French theologian, who emphasized in his teachings that it is how we live our faith, that is, a living in accord with the teachings of Christ Himself that wins the neighbor's approval.

In fact, the sermon's orientation was meant to raise awareness of the benefits of the Catholic school system in Texas. Beginning four centuries ago, during the time of Coronado, when Padre Juan de Padilla and Padre Juan de La Cruz were teaching Native Americans the fundamentals of the faith, the Catholic Church became active in spreading the faith in Texas. The old missionaries also taught the Native Americans quite a bit about agriculture and soil chemistry, even though it was not then so specialized.

In light of what the Church was teaching at the time in the field of education, Fr. Kirwin believed that statistics would convey the message. He referred to the Right Rev. John Timon as the first bishop of Texas, who Bishop John Mary Odin, a Vincentian father, immediately followed. Both were former presidents of St. Mary of the Barren's Seminary in Missouri. He was most eager to establish schools in the newly established Republic of Texas. Bishop Odin actually envisioned the Alamo as a Catholic college in a rebuilt form. This was evident from his report to his superior in Paris.

The time period surrounding the Civil War saw few public schools. Protestant religious denominations did not yet have their feet on the ground. Still, the Catholic Church in Galveston, San Antonio, Victoria, Brownsville, and Dallas had several religious orders running schools and academies at the grade and secondary school levels. The convent school left its impression on the convent girl, who was not always Catholic. These young ladies came to know the culture and refinement of their religious teachers. They themselves fostered this education.

Looking at the dioceses at that time, Dallas educated about 5400 children with thirteen academies for young ladies, thirty-eight parochial schools, and five training schools for nurses. Six thousand children were listed as under Catholic training and religious influence.

In the Galveston diocese, there was one seminary and a university at La Porte, and another college in Houston. These were for young men. There were eleven academies for young ladies and forty-six parochial schools. There were 9,608 young people under Catholic care.

In the Archdiocese of San Antonio, there was at that time one seminary, sixteen academies for young ladies, two colleges for women, and five colleges for boys. In total, the Catholic educational system had 14,174 young people under the care of the Archdiocese of San Antonio.

In the diocese of Corpus Christi, there was one college for boys and five academies for young ladies. This totaled 3,778 young people under the diocese of Corpus Christi's training.

In the diocese of El Paso at that time, there were 13 academies, 1 college for girls, and 13 parochial schools. In all, there were 4443 young people under the care of the Diocese of El Paso.

Looking back at the numbers, approximately 40,000 children in Texas were enrolled in the Catholic educational system. Referring to the literary writer Goethe, he noted that if you wish to see information in the life of the nation, it must first be introduced into the schools.

Catholic parents support the public school system through their taxes in addition to paying tuition to cover the cost of their own school system. The courses and texts conform to those used within the public school system. The Catholic school system insists that for the fully trained man and woman, there must be a knowledge of God and a practical realization of our duty and responsibility to Him. [76]

Persecution of the French Church

Fr. James Kirwin addressed the situation of the French Church as it stood at the beginning of the twentieth century. Following is a summary of his remarks made at Cathedral Hall in Galveston.

There is no question that the United States owes much to the French clergy. They came during the days when the Catholic Church was beginning to establish itself in this country. They came, living in poverty and peril. Some became martyrs for this land. One can recall the gift of the North American Martyrs. Some of these early French missionaries are buried in front of the Cathedral door in Galveston. They had sacrificed themselves during the scare of yellow fever. It

---

[76] "My Grace Is Sufficient for You." *Memoirs of Monsignor J.M. Kirwin.* George T. Elmendorf, Compiler, n.p.

would be wrong not to raise our voice in protest for what the French clergy are experiencing in their homeland at this time.

Our Father[77]

In 1789, during the French Revolution, all Church property was declared National, i.e., confiscated by the State. In 1791, the National Legislative body realized the injustice of the confiscation and declared that the state should pay for the salaries of the Catholic

[77] Our Father, Catholicfaithstore.com.

bishops and clergy. Napoleon entered into the Concordat of 1801. Napoleon and Pope Pius VII signed this agreement. Through this agreement, all Church property not already disposed of should be handed over to the bishops. In compensation for Church property already handed over, the salaries of bishops and priests should be paid for by the state. This was not a donation but a restitution. It was merely interest on a state debt. This agreement was a source of trouble and difficulty for over a century.

The liberty of teaching, as guaranteed by the Concordat and amplified by Napoleon III in 1852, was an object of hatred and alarm to these enemies of religion. To abrogate it, they introduced a sweeping measure which became law in July of 1901. This law of associations stated that no body of religious men or women could open or teach a school, or engage in any work of charity, without the Government's approval. Before the approval could be granted, the religious community had to give an inventory of its property. Sixty communities applied, and fifty-four communities were refused. Those who refused had their property taken by the State. As a result, three thousand schools closed; one million six hundred thousand children were deprived of educational facilities, and thousands of religious men and women were driven from their institutions and from their native land in the name of liberty by men who claimed themselves apostles of freedom, fraternity, and equality. Unfortunately, persecution did not stop here.

The 1905 French law on the separation of the Church and state followed. A separation bill was drafted and passed, which provided for the confiscation of all church property restored by the Concordat. This also included Church property obtained in the past one hundred years. The availability of the churches alone was allowed for a specified period of time, under conditions that were impossible to accept because the control of the Church was placed entirely in the hands of the government.

Naturally, the French bishops refused to accept such conditions.

At the end of this meeting, the chairman appointed a committee on resolutions. The following resolutions were then prepared and presented at the meeting. They were unanimously adopted. They read as follows:

The citizens of Galveston, in a mass meeting assembled, witnessed the pitiless expulsion from their homes of the Sisters of Charity, the despoilation of the churches, and the persecution of the people by the infidel Government of France:

RESOLVED, First: That we express our profound sympathy with the Holy Father and the Christians of France in their dire affliction.

Two: We brand the infamous action of the Government of France in expelling from their homes, and thereby depriving of the means of subsistence, thousands of religious women and Sisters of Charity, whose only crime was teaching the young duties most sacred, nursing the sick and infirm, giving solace and comfort to the feeble, aged and decrepit, caring for the little orphans and abandoned, ministering to the afflicted in the abodes of misery and pestilence, as an outrage against humanity, and as cruelty befitting only an uncivilized nation.

Third: We condemn the outrageous theft of Church property as unparalleled in the history of the civilized world, and as an injustice appealing to all mankind for redress.

Fourth: We denounce the shameless hypocrisy of those persecutors who talk of separation of Church and State, when they mean not separation merely, but enslavement and destruction of the Church.

Fifth: We resolve to transmit these resolutions to the papal secretary of state, to the aged cardinal of Paris, to President Roosevelt, and to the French ambassador in Washington.

Bishop Gallagher sent a cablegram to Cardinal Richard at Paris and Cardinal Merry del Val of Rome advising them of the action taken.[78]

[79]

[78] "Persecution of the French Church." *Memoirs of Monsignor J.M. Kirwin,* George T. Elmendorf, Compiler, n.p.

[79] Map of France, Dreamstime.com.

The Christian Soldier

Fr. Kirwin drew from St. Paul's letter to the Ephesians the perfect example of the Christian soldier. We are urged to put on the armor of God. Naturally, this does not address physical battles. As the scriptures remind us, our wrestling is not against flesh and blood. St. Paul was not addressing economic or material warfare. It is the conflict for heaven" against the deceits of the devil" (Eph 6:11).

One would have to say that the weapons of the Christian soldier can be utilized for the battle for heaven. St. Paul referred to having your loins girt about with truth. Put on the breastplate of justice. One's feet should be shod with the preparation of the Gospel of peace. The shield of faith is needed to extinguish the fiery darts of the wicked one. As St. Paul states in his letter to the Ephesians:

> Put on the armor of God so that you may be able to stand firm against the tactics of the devil. For our struggle is not with flesh and blood but with the principalities, with the powers, with the world rulers of this present darkness, with the evil spirits in the heavens. Therefore, put on the armor of God that you may be able to resist on the evil day, and, having done everything, to hold your ground. So stand fast with your loins girded in truth, clothed with righteousness as a breastplate, and your feet shod in readiness for the gospel of peace. In all circumstances, hold faith as a shield to quench all the flaming arrows of the evil one. And take the helmet of salvation and the sword of the Spirit, which is the word of God. (Eph 6:11-17)

One is called to have his loins girt about with truth. The truth is actually tied to the military academy. "Tell the truth." Do not depart from the ways of truth. Departing from it will lead to personal disgrace. The Christian soldier, as well as the individual on the battlefield, realizes its importance.

The Christian needs to clothe himself with the breastplate of justice. Thus, he has returned to the old forms of body armor in this world war. The Christian is called to pay his honest debts. If he fails, meaning that he falls into fraud and deceit, he is not dealing honestly with his fellow citizens. He is a scandal to those outside. His own conscience recognizes him as a hypocrite.

Your feet should be shod in readiness for the gospel of peace. Fr. Kirwin stated that trench feet and pedal weakness fill military hospitals and are the most frequent cause of rejection from army service. He sees a great number of Christians suffering from the same disease. They are not prepared to live the Gospel. When they meet trial and temptation, they easily succumb.

In all circumstances, hold faith as a shield. St. Paul reminded everyone of the necessity of faith. In other words, one cannot live the Gospel without faith. St. Paul insisted that faith is the only means of extinguishing the fiery darts hurled against us by the world, the flesh, and the devil.

Then the soldier wears the helmet, the helmet of salvation. The conflict at sea presents itself. Salvation depends upon our protection in the trenches. Thus, it is called the helmet of salvation. The Christian soldier must arm himself with prayer and the sacraments. Otherwise, he can easily be "picked off."

The sword of the Spirit is seen as the Word of God. It is there for our instruction and guidance. It is meant to be our firm hope when earthly comfort fails us. As Fr, Kirwin stated, "it is the only sword that can clear the way to the promised land, the hope of victory in heaven."[80]

> Put on the armor of God so that you may be able to stand firm against the tactics of the devil. For our struggle is not with flesh and blood but with the principalities, with the powers, with the world rulers of this present darkness, with the evil spirits in the heavens. Therefore, put on the armor of God that you may be able to resist on the evil day, and, having done everything, to hold your ground. So stand fast with your loins girded in truth, clothed with righteousness as a breastplate, and your feet shod in readiness for the gospel of peace. In all circumstances, hold faith as a shield to quench all the flaming arrows of the evil one. And take the helmet of salvation and the sword of the Spirit, which is the word of God. (Eph 6:11-17)

The Transfiguration

The Transfiguration is a frequently drawn upon Gospel passage. Fr. Kirwin tied it with the awareness of living the Christian life as we are called. Within the gospel account, Moses and Elijah,

---

[80]"The Christian Soldier," *Memoirs of Monsignor J.M. Kirwin,* George T. Elmendorf, Compiler, n.p.

representing the law and the prophets, appear with Christ. Peter, James, and John are awed by this scene. In fact, they are overpowered by it. The message can only be taken by way of vision and ecstasy. The three apostles will only fully put the message together after the Resurrection.

[81]

As Fr. Kirwin stated, the rest of the world at the bottom of the mountain continues its busy lifestyle. In other words, we allow the busyness of this world to distract us from that which is truly important.

Specifically, Fr. Kirwin spoke against the passion of lust and the exploitation of one's brother in business and other matters, the ills which St. Paul attacked in his first letter to the Thessalonians. Impurity and dishonesty can readily keep one away from the

[81] redletterChristians.org.

sacraments. Individuals may cry out that they have moved beyond the simple faith of children. They have doubts as adults that were not with them as children. The world's contacts have broadened their intellectual vision. While the trappings of the current age may differ, the struggle of today is still the same as in the time of St. Paul. He referred to the Thessalonican church in that regard. It is the will of God that we strive for holiness and, therefore, avoid immorality. We are further given the Holy Spirit as a wonderful guide in this regard (1 Thes 4:3-8).

Unfortunately, sexual impurity and commercial triumph can destroy the soul today as well as during the time of St. Paul. There needs to be a spirituality in place that protects the soul and guards the conscience. This is one major reason for the day of rest and worship that all might lift their vision to the matters of the Lord. Naturally, that lifting of one's mind to the ways of the Lord is borne forth with the image of the Transfiguration.

Raphael (1483-1520), the Italian artist of the High Renaissance, painted that unforgettable image of Christ on the mountain top. We, like Peter, James, and John, are drawn away from the temptations of this world. The Church calls us, like Peter, to hear the heavenly voices cry out, "Lord, it is good for us to be here!" (Mk 9:5). Christ's invitation has carried us away. It is within His presence that we seek His strength and grace to overcome those temptations that present themselves to us from the world. We are all called to hear that. Certainly, if coming into the presence of Christ at His invitation and witnessing His Transfiguration would not lift us from sexual desire and material gain, what would? Are we able to hear the voice of the heavenly Father, "This is My Beloved Son, Listen to Him"(Mk 9:7)?

It is the attendance at Mass and spiritual strengthening of the sacraments that is meant to enable us to refute those elements which are so readily available. As Fr. Kirwin preached, "Our actions must square with our principles. Cleanliness of life and honesty of purpose are both demanded." [82]

[83] The Transfiguration
Artist: Raffaello Sanzioda Urbino, known as Raphael

---

[82] "The Transfiguration," *Memoirs of Monsignor J.M. Kirwin,* George T. Elmendorf, Compiler, n.p.

[83]The Transfiguration, Artist: Raffaello Sanzioda Urbino, known as Raphael, Ncreguster.com.

Thy Sins Are Forgiven Thee (Mt 9:2)

Fr. Kirwin stated that the historic Church was proud of the ninth chapter of Matthew. Those who have faith in the divinity of Christ follow Him. The beginning of that chapter conveys Jesus forgiving the sins of a paralyzed man. Some scribes immediately assumed Jesus was blaspheming. "This man is blaspheming," Jesus responded with, "Why do you harbor evil thoughts? Which is easier to say, your sins are forgiven or to say, arise and walk?" (Mt 9:5) Questioning of His sincerity would not suffice. Rather, Jesus chose to prove His divinity and His power. But that you may know that the Son of Man has authority on earth to forgive sins, He then said to the paralytic, "Rise, pick up your stretcher and go home." He arose and went home. "When the crowds saw this, they were struck with awe and glorified God who had given such authority to human beings" (Mt 9:6-8).

The scriptures verified that those with a firm faith in the divinity of Christ knew that Christ can forgive sins by the spoken word or through delegated agents. As Fr. Kirwin preached, the proof of delegation is always rightly demanded.

Christ chose to pick twelve ignorant men from the lakeside and the hills of Galilee. He paid the penalty for sin on Calvary. He returned, triumphing over death from the tomb. He then delegated power to these men.

He appeared to them the first day of the week, which was Sunday, and stood in their midst, "Peace be with you.'When Christ said this, He showed them His hands and His side and said again, 'Peace be with you. As the Father has sent Me, I send you.' When He uttered this, He breathed on them and said to them, 'Receive the Holy Spirit. Whose sins you forgive are forgiven them, and whose sins you retain are retained'" (John 20:21-23).

Thus, Fr. Kirwin testified that the apostles received the power to forgive sins, and that their successors likewise have this power. In the latter part of Matthew's gospel, that verification is brought forth, "teaching them to observe all that I have commanded you. And behold, I am with you always, until the end of the age" (Mt 28:20).

Every baptized Catholic who avails himself of the grace of the sacrament of Penance knows that he must present himself in sincere faith, with a sorrow for the sins committed, and a firm purpose to avoid those sins in the future and, likewise, the occasion of sin in the future. Then, just as surely as the paralyzed man was cured of his physical ailment and walked upright, so certainly do the words of absolution by the priest cure the soul of sin. As the priest has told the penitent many times over, "Son, be of good heart, thy sins are forgiven thee." Like Longfellow's maiden Evangeline, we know the comfort of the sacrament of Penance:[84]

> A celestial brightness—a more ethereal beauty—
> Shone on her face and encircled her form, when, after confession,
> Homeward serenely she walked with God's benediction upon her.[85]

---

[84] Fr. James Kirwin, "Thy Sins Are Forgiven Thee (Mt 9:2)". *Memoirs of Monsignor J.M. Kirwin.* George T. Elmendorf, Compiler, n.p.

[85] Henry Wadsworth Longfellow, "Evangeline—A Tale of Acadie 1847," Maine Historical Society. hwlongfellow.org.

[86] [87]

The Loaves and the Fish

In the gospel of Mark, the story of the multiplication of the loaves and fish is addressed. It is quite apparent that Jesus is moved with compassion for the crowd following Him, for they wish to hear

[86] Stanthonyofsaranac.org.

[87] "You Are Forgiven," Stmaryoticandhoc.org.

His message, yet have no opportunity to partake of food, especially in the terrain they find themselves in.

This miracle is found in all four Gospels, yet is questioned by many, who seek a natural explanation for the multiplication of the food at hand. Fr. Kirwin noted that the power of God is seen in the creation story. Christ readily dispensed with the laws of nature by way of the multiplication of the loaves and fish. The divinity of Christ is plainly visible in many other instances.

As mentioned earlier, Christ is moved with compassion for the people, for they appeared as sheep without a shepherd. So, He taught them and also provided for their bodily needs. In the specific example, the crowd has been with Christ for some time and is therefore quite tired. Christ's compassion for the crowd is readily apparent. There was fear in the crowd of five thousand that they would faint on the way to their own homes as they were "in a deserted place and it was already very late" (Mk 6:34). Where could such an amount of bread be found in the wilderness? So, Jesus asked the redundant question as to whether there was anyone there who could feed them. Naturally, with the size of the crowd, there was not. As the Gospel writer states, He already knew what He would do. He had them recline for the multiplication of the loaves and the fish.

Fr. Kirwin immediately moved to the Bread of Life Discourse. Naturally, his purpose as celebrant of the Mass was to relate the passage to the reception of the Eucharist at Mass. "I am the living Bread from heaven; whoever eats this Bread will live forever; and the Bread that I will give is my Flesh for the life of the world (John 6:51). We as Roman Catholics believe that the promise which is made in the above verse is fulfilled at the Last Supper. The reception of the

Eucharist remains, that is, it is continued through the ages "even until the consummation of the world." This gift of the Eucharist continues to be offered through the ordained Priesthood of Jesus Christ; "Do this in commemoration of Me" (Lk 22:19).

Fr. Kirwin looked upon the Eucharist as the sacrament of love. Jesus did have compassion upon the multitudes. Fr. Kirwin was thinking of the "war-torn multitudes of the world" and likewise of the passage in the psalms "justice and peace shall kiss" (Psalm 85:11). He, at that moment, was praying that charity and harmony would take their place "in the parliament of man." [88]

[89]

John 6:51

---

[88]Fr. James Kirwin, "The Loaves and the Fish." *Memoirs of Monsignor J.M. Kirwin*, George T. Elmendorf, Compiler, n.p.

[89]"I Am the Living Bread that came down from heaven. Whoever eats this bread will live forever". John 6:51. Catholiccurrent.org.

Chapter Seven

The Knights of Columbus

The Dream of Fr. Michael McGivney

Michael McGivney was born August 12, 1852, in Westbury, Connecticut, to an Irish immigrant family. His father made enough of a living in metal molding to support the family and pay for Michael's seminary studies. Michael studied at the College of St. Hyacinth in Quebec. He proceeded on to Our Lady of the Angels Seminary in Niagara Falls and St. Mary's Seminary run by the Jesuits in Montreal. However, when Michael's father died suddenly in 1873, Michael had to leave his seminary studies and go to work to support his mother and the remainder of the family. Realizing that Michael might easily land back in the Jesuit seminary, the bishop of Hartford, Connecticut, offered Michael a full scholarship to the seminary in Baltimore. Actually, at that point in his life, Michael truly wished for the priesthood but had ruled out the life of a Jesuit. He was ordained by Archbishop James Gibbon on December 22, 1877, in Baltimore.[1]

Fr. McGivney first served as Curate at St. Mary's Church in New Haven, Connecticut. He worked with youth as he was the chaplain of St. Joseph's Young Men's Society within the parish. Unfor-

[1] Michael O'Neill, "Blessed Michael McGivney, Parish Priest and Founder of the Knights of Columbus," *They Might Be Saints on the Path to Sainthood in America* (Irondale, Alabama: EWTN Publishing, Inc., 2021), 55-59.

tunately, at that time, many men stopped attending Church around the age of 20. They were either working or engaging in their own amusements on a Sunday morning. Fr. McGivney visited the ill, the jail, and taught catechism classes, among other parish responsibilities. All of this ministry led him to realize the need for a Catholic group with a strong fraternal element. He wished to prevent Catholics from joining condemned secret societies, yet, at the same time, provide the means to protect families during times of sickness and death of the breadwinner, due to TB and other common illnesses.[2]

Fr. McGivney was known for helping a family through the loss of a loved one. He was gravely struck by the loss of the breadwinner in the Downes family after the birth of their fourteenth child. The father had left no savings, and they had the eldest son in the seminary. This eldest son left the seminary to support the family. The state of Connecticut wished to make sure the mother and children were provided for. At the first hearing in the probate court, Edward Downes, Junior, who had left the seminary to support the family, convinced the judge that he could keep the father's business going and provide for the younger children. The judge was concerned about the three next oldest, Alfred, nineteen, George, seventeen, and Joseph, fourteen. A guardian had to be found for each of these boys who was of good character and would take full responsibility. In addition, a $1,500 bond was set for each boy. The

---

[2] Christopher Kauffman, "McGivney, Michael J. (1852-1890)," *The Encyclopedia of American Catholic History,* ed. Michael Glazier and Thomas J. Shelley (Collegeville, Minnesota: A Michael Glazier Book, the Liturgical Press, 1997), 1:881.

extended family found guardians for George and Joseph, but not Alfred. At the second hearing, the judge accepted guardianship of the two younger boys. When it came to Alfred, Fr. McGivney stood and stated that he did not have the required money but had the pledge of a retired grocer, Patrick McKiernan, to provide surety. Thus, if Fr. McGivney failed in his guardianship, the grocer would pay the "penal sum" of $1,500. The judge accepted the arrangement.[3]

Fr. McGivney, shortly after, met with several men of his parish to form a Catholic fraternal benefit society to prevent this situation from happening again. This would provide a social group and an insurance program. There were already several secret societies in existence, such as the Freemasons, who were anti-Catholic. While there were some Catholic societies around, Fr. McGivney wished to found a Catholic and American society. They began with a motto of Charity and Unity. Fraternity was later added. Fr. McGivney invited all the pastors in Connecticut to form local chapters. The primary aim was to prevent people from joining secret societies. Secondly, he wished to gain members of the faith to provide support in case of sickness and possible death within a family. Thus, at the age of 29, he wished to establish a Catholic fraternal society which would take pride in the American Catholic heritage. While he initially served as supreme secretary, by June 15 of 1884, he was elected Supreme Chaplain, a role more in line with his priestly duties.[4]

---

[3] "Blessed Michael McGivney," *They Might Be Saints on the Path to Sainthood in America*, 60-61.

[4] Ibid., 62-63, and Christopher Kauffman, "McGivney, Michael J. (1852-1890)," *The Encyclopedia of American Catholic History*, ed. Michael

As Fr. McGivney moved from St. Mary's Parish to St. Thomas Parish within the diocese of Hartford, Connecticut, he was given a fond farewell from his parishioners at St. Mary's. The *New Haven Evening Register* reported that he was an energetic and hardworking priest. He continued to work on expanding the Knights in his new parish. He became well known in Connecticut. While the Knights had a rather slow beginning, they grew rapidly within a matter of time.[5]

Unfortunately, Fr. McGivney contracted pneumonia in January of 1890. He received treatment in New York, but the disease overcame him on August 14, 1890. He was eulogized by many at the funeral, including Edward Downes. Fr. McGivney was only 38 years of age at the time of his passing.[6]

He is now recognized as Blessed within the steps for canonization. The miracle necessary for that step came about when a mother of twelve children in 2014 was told her expectant baby would not survive. The family turned to Fr. McGivney in prayer. They had a devotion to Fr. McGivney, as the father worked for the Knights of Columbus. They went on a pilgrimage to Fatima. Upon returning, the ultrasound results showed they expected a healthy baby. With those results, the little boy was named Michael after his patron. Fr. McGivney had been declared Venerable in 2008.

Glazier and Thomas J. Shelley (Collegeville, Minnesota: A Michael Glazier Book, the Liturgical Press, 1997), 1:881.

[5] "Blessed Michael McGivney," *They Might Be Saints on the Path to Sainthood in America,* 64.

[6] Kauffman, "McGivney, Michael J. (1852-1890)," *The Encyclopedia of American Catholic History, 1:882.*

Following the approval of this miracle in 2020, he was declared Blessed. [7]

[8] Fr. Michael McGivney, Founder of the Knights of Columbus

Highlights of the History behind the Knights

The Knights of Columbus chose Christopher Columbus as their patron. They added fraternity and patriotism in 1885 and 1900, respectively, to their founding principles.

By the early twentieth century, the Knights of Columbus had expanded into Mexico, the Philippines, Cuba, and Panama. During this time period, they also traveled to college campuses to establish Chapters of the Knights. The first was formed at Notre Dame

---

[7] "Blessed Michael McGivney," *They Might Be Saints on the Path to Sainthood in America, 64-65.*

[8] Fr. Michael McGivney, Founder of the Knights of Columbus, Catholictradition.org.

University. Catholic U received a grant for a study in American History. The Knights also raised to the Fourth Degree some 2,000 knights in New York and Boston.

During World War I and World War II, the Knights provided havens of rest for members of all faiths and nationalities. The Christopher Columbus Memorial Fountain was established in Washington, D.C. in 1912. Over 400,000 men joined the Knights after World War I.

The Knights assisted individuals in finding work after World War I. They fought against the anti-Catholic sentiment found within the Ku Klux Klan and other nativist groups. They published literature on the contributions of Jewish Americans, African Americans, and German Americans. Knights met with President Calvin Coolidge in an attempt to overcome the bigotry against Catholics in Mexico in the 1920s and 1930s. The Knights fought alongside Pope Pius XI in the 1930's against the spread of Communism.

The Knights celebrated fifty years of service with the unveiling of a statue of James Cardinal Gibbons, a strong supporter of the Knights, in 1932 in Washington, D.C.

During and after the years when World War II raged, the Knights launched a Crusade for the Preservation and Promotion of American ideals. A trust fund was established for the children of servicemen who were lost in the war. The Philippines experienced a tremendous membership growth.

The Knights were very influential in adding "under God" to the Pledge of Allegiance in 1954. The Knights contributed a million dollars toward the building of a bell tower at the National Shrine of the Immaculate Conception in Washington, D.C. The Order financed the microfilming of materials from the Vatican Library. These microfilms became available at St. Louis University.

The Knights published a booklet on the encyclical *Humanae Vitae, an attempt to promote marriage and to clarify* the Catholic theology of procreation. The Supreme Council headquarters chose to construct four 320-foot towers, each representing one of the four principles of the Knights: charity, unity, fraternity, and patriotism.

Among other initiatives of the Knights, they celebrated the fifth centenary of the evangelization of the New World. They also financed several very worthwhile educational initiatives. Among them was a scholarship fund for Catholic seminaries and universities, and further, the establishment of a North American campus of the Pontifical John Paul II Institute for Studies on Marriage and Family.

The Order began a restoration of St. Mary's Church, the parish that Fr. Michael McGivney served in as his first assignment. The Knights underwrote the expenses for the filming of the first visit of Pope John Paul II to the United States. The Order chose to underwrite the expense for the cleaning of the 65,000 square foot façade of St. Peter's Basilica. It was the first time it had been cleaned in 350 years. The Knights took on several other restoration projects at St. Peter's.

After the terrorist attack on 9/11, the Knights provided aid to the victims and their families. This was also done for the victims of Hurricane Katrina in Louisiana. Pope John Paul II canonized 25 martyrs from Mexico in 2000. Six of them were members of the Knights of Columbus. The Knights of Columbus Museum opened in 2001 in New Haven, Connecticut. One hundred thousand prayer books were printed for members of the military in the year 2003. Two years later, the Knights sent 2,000 wheelchairs to people with disabilities in Afghanistan and elsewhere as part of its global wheelchair mission.

The Order continues to advocate for Christians in the Middle East. They provided over 1,000 ultrasound machines to pregnancy centers across this country. The St. John Paul II Shrine was established in Washington, D.C. They partnered with Catholic Relief Services in providing aid to the residents of Haiti after an earthquake in 2010. The Knights have supplied needed funds for those fleeing persecution in Iraq and other areas where religious freedom is denied. The Knights have bestowed their Gaudium et Spes Award on several individuals, including the Little Sisters of the Poor. [9]

[10] Emblem of the Knights of Columbus

[9] Knights of Columbus.org.

The Knights of Columbus in Texas—Establishment of the Fourth Degree

The Knights of Columbus have been very active in Texas for many years. Msgr. James Kirwin was a constant supporter of the Knights ever since he arrived in Texas.

It took a bit of time for the Knights to organize themselves within the Houston area. The Catholic population in 1905 was rather small. There were actually 250 men present for this initial meeting. They came from Sherman, Fort Worth, Dallas, Galveston, Beaumont, Denison, Austin, and El Paso. There was, in addition, a large number from San Antonio and El Paso. There were also prominent visitors from other states. [11]

The first assemblage of the Knights took place on Sunday, March 26, at 7:30 am in the Odd Fellows' Hall with the exemplification of the first degree under the auspices of the Galveston Council. At that time, it was located at 420 Texas Avenue. The Knights and candidates then marched to Annunciation Church for a High Mass. Fr. V. Grattan sang it. The pastor of Annunciation, Fr. Thomas Hennessy, delivered the sermon. He welcomed the group and complimented the Knights for their work. The second degree was exemplified at 1:30 pm. The third-degree exemplification followed

---

[10]"Emblem of the Knights of Columbus," 110 Knights of Columbus ideas.

[11] William H. Oberste, *Knights of Columbus in Texas 1902-1952* (Austin, TX: Von Boeckmann-Jones Company, 1951), 32.

this. A banquet was served in the Auditorium of Incarnate Word Academy by the ladies of Annunciation Parish. The First Toast was "Our Church and our Order," responded to by Fr. James Kirwin. Other toasts and responses followed, and music was provided throughout the evening. At the close, in accordance with the patriotic custom of the Knights, they sang the national anthem. Members of the Houston Council met on Monday evening, March 27, to elect officers. The Knights of Columbus were soon organized in all the principal cities in Texas. [12]

There are actually four degrees to the Knights of Columbus. Each degree emphasizes one of the four core virtues: charity, unity, fraternity, and patriotism. To enter the Knights, a person must be a minimum of 18 years of age, a Catholic in good standing, and recommended by a fellow knight. Once the prospective member is approved, he participates in a first-degree ceremony. The second and third degrees do not have specific requirements. The ceremonies typically follow one another. [13]

A familiar sight among the Knights is the attire used by members in full regalia. Some years back, it was assumed there would be a multiplicity of degrees within the Knights. However, the conferring of additional degrees beyond the fourth was rejected by Bishop Harkins, Bishop of the Province. Since then, the Fourth Degree is the highest Degree within the Order. Admittance to the Fourth Degree of the Order is open to every Third Degree Knight of Columbus who is recommended as a Knight in good standing and,

---

[12] Oberste, *Knights of Columbus in Texas 1902-1952*, 32-35.

[13] Knights of Columbus, Msgr. George A. Wilhelm Assembly, #1094.

further, as a good and devoted Catholic. The Fourth Degree was officially adopted by the Order in 1899. The Fourth Degree ceremony emphasized patriotism. [14]

In Texas, the Fourth Degree was established when members received it on May 31, 1906. The ceremony was held in Denver, Colorado. Fr. Kirwin was the celebrant of the Mass. Bishop Nicholas Matz, Bishop of Denver, presided at the Church function. The sermon was preached by Fr. Joseph Lynch from Dallas. He preached on "The Southern Knight." The first exemplification of the Fourth Degree in Texas took place in Dallas on February 22, 1907. A second exemplification took place in Dallas on November 26, 1908, and then again in February 1909. Fr. Kirwin was at the 1909 ceremonial. By this time, there were over four hundred Fourth Degree members in Texas. The state of Texas encompassed what was referred to as the Guadalupe Province. The Fourth Degree Assemblies met annually to renew their obligations. They usually contributed to some worthy cause. Members of the Fourth Degree have been interested in providing for the preservation of the old missions and sites of old churches to advance the history of the Church in Texas. [15]

Texas A & M Chapel

The year was 1923. A delegate from the Bryan Council, L.W. Warren, took the floor at the Austin Convention to explain the great need of Catholics at Texas A & M University for a chapel. Fr.

---

[14] Oberste, *Knights of Columbus in Texas 1902-1952*, 227-228.

[15] Ibid., 227-232.

Gleissner, the pastor at St. Joseph's in Bryan, took the floor himself to explain that students had to walk six miles, sometimes in the mud, to get to Mass. That was the distance to St. Joseph's Church in Bryan. The proposal received unanimous approval from the delegates. Fr. James Kirwin asked delegates to stand up if they were willing to raise $100.00 for the proposal. Fr. Kirwin stated that the Catholic Church Extension Society would make up the difference. The Minutes did not show that the Extension Society was aware of the proposal. The Convention closed without a Resolution. However, State Deputy J.I. Driscoll, at the Laredo Convention in 1924, reminded delegates that the Bryan Council had made an appeal for a Chapel for students attending A & M, and, thus far, the plea had gone unheeded. A recommendation was made that the State deputy confer with the Bishop of Galveston. After obtaining his approval and recommendations, steps should be taken to proceed with erecting the chapel. This recommendation at the Laredo Convention created new interest. [16]

Unfortunately, the Knights did not have the funds at the time to build a chapel. However, the cause was considered so worthy that individual members of the Knights from Cameron, Texarkana, Orange, Hallettsville, West, Santa Maria, Port Arthur, and, of course, Bryan made individual donations to buy land for the chapel. The $1,000 collected enabled the purchase of a site north of the campus. Bishop Byrne asked the State Deputy Driscoll of the Council to consult with Fr. Gleissner regarding the site. Fr. Gleissner, upon hearing of the property in the summer of 1926, found the location quite

---

[16] Ibid., 227-232.

suitable. By April 1927, the proposed chapel, only a dream for Fr. Gleissner, had become a reality. Fr. Gleissner saw it as the happiest day of his life. Bishop Byrne dedicated the chapel on April 24, 1927. He thanked the Knights for a generous contribution to the diocese of Galveston. [17]

At that Mass, the state chaplain, the Reverend J.S. Murphy, was the celebrant. The deacon and subdeacon, respectively, were the Reverend F. O'Brien of Texarkana, past state chaplain, and the Reverend William Blakeslee, CSP, Chaplain of the Newman Club of Texas University. The Reverend J. Rapp of Sacred Heart Church in Houston was the Master of Ceremonies. Six cadets of A & M served as Acolytes. The choirs of St. Joseph's Church in Bryan and Immaculate Conception Church in Houston provided the singing. [18]

The Mass was followed by "a real Texas barbecue." The President of A & M, President Walton, complimented the Knights for their great interest in the Aggies and also as the first group to build a chapel at A & M. When Fr. Gleissner stood up, he received an overwhelming ovation. He spoke with tremendous gratitude. It had only taken four years to bring about a twenty-year dream. Fr. Gleissner came to every Convention to report on the spiritual good done through the Chapel. That is not even mentioning the number of Aggies who joined the Knights. In 1948, the Newman Club reported that a larger Church and Newman Hall were needed. Bishop Reicher, Bishop of Austin, authorized the necessary expenditures for a chapel, student center, and resident priest, in addition to

---

[17]"Monsignor Gleissner's Diamond Jubilee to the Priesthood Celebrated," *Southern Messenger*, December 1, 1949.

[18]Oberste, *Knights of Columbus in Texas 1902-1952*, 152.

classrooms for religious instruction. The bishop saw these as essential. It all began with St. Mary's Chapel, established by the Knights. [19]

[20] Catholic Center in College Station "Aggie Land"

Historical Commission of the Knights

The state of Texas has enjoyed a colorful history for many decades. More than sixty missions existed in the Lone Star state at the time of the friars. The missions became important through the crown of Spain and the Church. The state convention meeting in Yoakum in 1922 passed a resolution calling for efforts to commemorate and perpetuate the events that occurred in these missions. A committee was appointed with the blessing of Bishop C.E. Byrne of Galveston by the State Convention to confer with the

---

[19] Ibid., 156-159.

[20] Theeagle.com.

Texas Bishops with a view to marking substantially those places connected with the introduction of the Catholic Faith in Texas. However, they realized a marking was not sufficient.[21]

The Knights pursued the publication of the history through the efforts of the Honorable William Blakeslee. They referred to an "imperative necessity" for a Catholic History of Texas. Thus, in 1927, a historical commission was created. This commission referred to the "stupendous labors" of the late lamented Very Rev. J.M. Kirwin, Vicar General of the Diocese of Galveston, whose tireless energies to discover and reveal the truth about the history of Texas and its "Christian civilization" certainly were greatly appreciated. The efforts of the "revered missionary," Fr. P. F. Parisot, OMI, and his associates in gathering the facts to form a part of the History of Texas were certainly appreciated. This was, in addition to the work of Fr. Joseph P. Lynch, who was the Metropolitan of the diocese of Dallas. A "powerful plea" had arisen from the assembly of the Knights who met in Houston several years earlier, asking that the great monuments of civilization erected by the Catholic missionaries be preserved in fact and in history for the current and future generations.[22]

It was the belief of the Executive Committee of the Knights of Columbus that there would be a definite course of study showing the influence of the Catholic Church in the early history of Texas, and that major libraries could be called upon, specifically the Bexar Archives, the University of Texas, the Paulist Fathers at the Newman

---

[21] Oberste, *Knights of Columbus in Texas 1902-1952*, 165-167.

[22] Ibid., 167-169.

Center, among other sites. It was further thought that the study would take several years. The Supreme Council of the Knights amended its Charter, enabling it to engage in various activities. It further established a Historical Commission. This enabled the Texas State Council of the Knights of Columbus to undertake a Catholic History of Texas. The meeting took place in Austin in May of 1923. The delegates received a report on the anti-Catholic literature distributed throughout Texas. Meetings were held in Laredo and Dallas.[23]

At the earlier suggestion of Msgr. Kirwin, the assistance of Dr. Peter Guilday was attained. Dr. Guilday from Catholic U brought forth for publication in 1936 a centennial History of the State of Texas. Msgr. Kirwin had already outlined the Introduction in his history of the diocese of Galveston. In accord with the recommendation of Dr. Guilday, Fr. Paul Foik, CSC, from St. Edward's University, was appointed permanent Chairman of the project. He gave the remainder of his life to working on the Historical Commission.[24]

Before the 1936 planned publication, the Historical Commission was reorganized in the 1920's. Priest Historians from the various dioceses were added to the membership of the Commission. St. Edward's University became the custodian of the Knights of Columbus Archives.[25]

The first three volumes on the Mission Era were written by Rev. Dr. Francis Borgia Steck, O.F.M. Fr. Steck was then called upon to

---

[23] Ibid., 169-172.

[24] Ibid., 173-177.

[25] Ibid., 177-200.

take on a Professorship of Latin American History at Catholic University of America. Therefore, by mutual agreement, his contract was terminated. Dr. Carlos E. Castañeda continued the writing. Dr. Castañeda was familiar with the archival material and certainly possessed an excellent knowledge of the Spanish language. He would be writing a history of the Church and of Texas. Initially, it was a part-time project for him, as he served as a professor of the history of Spain and Latin America at the University of Texas. He did, however, spend every available moment on this project. The first five volumes were on the Mission Era. Since he was invited to serve on the Fair Employment Commission for President Roosevelt, volume VI was delayed. It was published in 1950 under the Subtitle "The Fight for Freedom." It provides the History of the Church in Texas from 1810 through 1836. It was decided that the final volume would carry the study of the Church up to 1950. It was entitled "Growth of the Church." Fr. Foik edited the first four of the seven volumes of the study. Unfortunately, he died of "a long and lingering illness" on March 1, 1941. Thus, the remainder of the volumes were edited by Fr. James P. Gibbons, CSC, from St. Edward's University. [26]

In anticipation of the termination of the Historical Commission's project, with the publication of all seven volumes of Our Catholic Heritage, some suggested fostering a continued interest in the history of the Church in Texas. This could be done independently of the Historical Commission through the Texas Catholic Historical Society. The Church's hierarchy in Texas would

---

[26] Ibid., 177-200.

sponsor this Society. This would, therefore, give it "authority, permanence and legal standing." Thus, the Bishops of Texas, at a meeting of the hierarchy in San Antonio on April 8, 1947, formed the Texas Catholic Historical Society, Inc., and approved a tentative charter. The articles of incorporation covered a term of fifty years. The directors of the corporation were the Bishop Ordinaries of the state of Texas. In Article II of the incorporation document, it is stated that the purpose for which the corporation is formed is the "support and furtherance of historical studies, the discovery, collection, and preservation of material relating to the history of the Roman Catholic Church in the state of Texas, and sponsoring activities" which would carry out those objectives. [27]

It was further hoped that a historical review might be established to allow historians of the state to bring their own written contributions to the reading public. The archives from the material used for the writing of *Our Catholic Heritage* were merged, with the consent of the Knights of Columbus, with a Texana collection of Bishop Laurence FitzSimon from Amarillo at Price College, and conducted by the Christian Brothers in Amarillo, Texas. This provided one site for anyone who needed to research the history of the Church in Texas. Bishop FitzSimon has, since then, made several trips to France to collect "authentic information" about the early French missionaries working in Texas. [28]

---

[27] Ibid., 200-202.

[28] Ibid., 202-206.

[29] Dr. Carlos Castañeda, Author of *Our Catholic Heritage*

[29] "Dr. Carlos Castañeda," Humanities, Texas.

[30] Right Reverend C.E.Byrne, Bishop of Galveston
A Great Promoter of the Knights of Columbus

[30]Right Reverend C.E. Byrne, Bishop of Galveston, A Great Promoter of the Knights of Columbus, *Memoirs of Monsignor J.M. Kirwin*, George T. Elmendorf. Compiler. n.p.

Sermons of Msgr. Kirwin Dealing with the Knights of Columbus

In Commemoration of Columbus Day

Fr. Kirwin, in noting one of the readings for October 15, 1916, specifically 1 Cor 1:4-8, highlights in particular the gratitude St. Paul shares with his readers. That gratitude is grounded in what we have received from Christ. This is not uncommon with his Christocentric theology. Columbus is seen as "the bearer of the Christ." After the cross, there is no more sacred symbol than the American flag. This statement frequently flowed from Msgr—Kirwin's pen and lips. The Catholic faith had much to do with Columbus as a Christ bearer, for he engendered others to move that cross of Christ into the New World, whether it be an Isabella, the queen who financed the voyage, the Franciscans who boarded these three ships, or a map maker who ultimately provided the name of the continent. As the Celebrant stated, "it is not enough to carry the principles of the Catholic faith in your heart, you must externalize them and carry the message to others who 'sit in darkness and the shadow of the valley of death.'"

One can travel further into history and note the blood of missionaries, some of whom became martyrs, who traveled along the Canadian borders, in Florida, and along the slopes of the Rocky Mountains. In all of these areas, the blood and sweat of the missionaries and martyrs fertilized the land with the seeds of the Catholic faith. Their efforts are evident on the prairies, along the rivers, at the mission of Guadalupe, and at the missions of Texas. Antonio Margil established the mission of Guadalupe near

Nacogdoches. Three Franciscans were martyred among the Tiguas in 1582.

The greatest influence within this exploration and development of civilization was the Catholic priest. One may bring to mind the missions circling San Antonio, his efforts along the Brazos de Dios. The first permanent structure is found within the diocese of El Paso at Ysleta del Sur. As Fr. Kirwin illustrated, Catholics led the way as one perceives the trace of the missionary's footsteps."Not a land was found, not a mountain crossed, not a stream forded, but Catholics led the way."

If one were to move on to one of the thirteen original colonies, Maryland, the importance of religious freedom cannot be underestimated. George Washington, the father of our country, certainly recognized the significance of religious freedom. Archbishop John Carroll, in drawing upon the image of a tree, wished it to become sturdy and deep-rooted in the soil, "yielding abundantly the fruits of sanctification." Fr. Kirwin rejoiced at the development of the Church in America for the sake of the country itself. The Church contributes to the stability of the nation. She is a friend of law and order and a stern opponent of anarchy and oppression. Because of her conservative spirit, she provides a source of strength to the nation.

The educated Catholic does not give any special claim to service in America, for Catholics and Protestants worked together. They stood side by side in seeking liberty for all people. They have lived together, worked together, and voted together. They must see each other as friends. They must work together to maintain constitutional guarantees and to correct social evils. They do not permit uncharitable, un-Christian, and certainly un-American appeals to prejudice, passion, or ill feeling to disturb their friendly relations.

In Commemoration of Columbus Day

Fr. Kirwin, in noting one of the readings for October 15, 1916, specifically 1 Cor 1:4-8, highlights the gratitude St. Paul shares with his readers. That gratitude is grounded in what we have received from Christ. This is not uncommon with his Christocentric theology. Columbus is seen as "the bearer of the Christ." After the cross, there is no more sacred symbol than the American flag. This statement frequently flowed from Msgr. Kirwin's pen and lips. The Catholic faith had much to do with Columbus as a Christ bearer, for he engendered others to move that cross of Christ into the New World, whether it be an Isabella, the queen who financed the voyage, the Franciscans who boarded these three ships, or a map maker who ultimately provided the name of the continent. As the Celebrant stated, "it is not enough to carry the principles of the Catholic faith in your heart, you must externalize them and carry the message to others who 'sit in darkness and the shadow of the valley of death.'"

One can travel further into history and note the blood of missionaries, some of whom became martyrs, who traveled along the Canadian borders, in Florida, and along the slopes of the Rocky Mountains. In all of these areas, the blood and sweat of the missionaries and martyrs fertilized the land with the seeds of the Catholic faith. Their efforts are evident on the prairies, along the rivers, at the mission of Guadalupe, and at the missions of Texas. Antonio Margil established the mission of Guadalupe near

Nacogdoches. Three Franciscans were martyred among the Tiguas in 1582.

The greatest influence within this exploration and development of civilization was the Catholic priest. One may bring to mind the missions circling San Antonio, his efforts along the Brazos de Dios. The first permanent structure is found within the diocese of El Paso at Ysleta del Sur. As Fr. Kirwin illustrated, Catholics led the way as one perceives the trace of the missionary's footsteps."Not a land was found, not a mountain crossed, not a stream forded, but Catholics led the way."

If one were to move on to one of the thirteen original colonies, Maryland, the importance of religious freedom cannot be underestimated. George Washington, the father of our country, certainly recognized the importance of religious freedom. Archbishop John Carroll, in drawing upon the image of a tree, wished it to become sturdy and deep-rooted in the soil, "yielding abundantly the fruits of sanctification." Fr. Kirwin rejoiced at the development of the Church in America for the sake of the country itself. The Church contributes to the stability of the nation. She is a friend of law and order and a stern opponent of anarchy and oppression. Because of her conservative spirit, she provides a source of strength to the nation.

The educated Catholic does not give any special claim to service in America, for Catholics and Protestants worked together. They stood side by side in seeking liberty for all people. They have lived together, worked together, and voted together. They must see each other as friends. They must work together to maintain constitutional guarantees and to correct social evils. They do not permit uncharitable, un-Christian, and certainly un-American appeals to prejudice, passion, or ill feeling to disturb their friendly relations.

It is the task of the Catholic Church to raise the moral level of humanity. Fr. Kirwin turned to the Knights of Columbus and asked these men to uphold the Catholic code. The old order changed as he stated, but God Himself does not change. The touch of God renews the face of the earth. The character, mission, and doctrine of the Church do not change, as they are of God. Yet her dress, her step, her carriage, and her mode of dealing with nations must vary with the times.

Our fathers brought about the past, yet it is up to us to bring about the future. "The Church today is living, thriving, flourishing, and if it would triumph, it must be through its present ability to meet and solve and conquer the needs of humanity." Fr. Kirwin called upon the words of St. Anselm," He who lives for truth and justice lives for Christ." Since we live in a country that is a republic, it is founded upon the virtue of its citizens. This foundation cannot be weakened or destroyed without threatening the entire social structure. The early founding fathers were imbued with strong religious principles. From this, virtue can be fostered.

Fr. Kirwin stated that we are unfortunately living without God in our world. "Our love of principle and moral conviction seems to be growing weaker." When we are dominated by greed, we become reckless in how we obtain money.

Fortunately, some speak out against socialism, including the Knights of Columbus. Materialism, infidelity, and other forms of irreligion tear down but do not build up. Much depends on the Catholic laity in building up the future of the Church in the United

States. Her mission today, as at its inception, is to teach all nations to preach the Gospel to every creature. God's arm is by no means shortened. We are called to be good Catholics and then true Americans. We are called to be models of civic virtue. We are summoned to inform ourselves that we make an intelligent defense of our faith. "The Catholic can best answer lies by living the truth and showing to all the world that his standard of faith and morals is the stainless banner of the crucified Christ." That is true even when we find the malicious darts of prejudice.

Fr. Kirwin noted the words of St. Paul in his first letter to the Corinthians, "The greatest of these is charity." It has been transmitted not only in words but deep in the hearts of men. In referring to all the wonders in God's creation, "Thou hast made him a little less than the angels." (Psalm 8:5, Heb 2:7) Real charity bends the strong to serve the weak; it keeps the mother by the cradle; it puts the Sisters of Charity by the cot of pestilence; it chastens wealth by service of the poor.

A Knight advances to higher planes of service as he states in his pledge:

The house from which the heavens are fed,
The old, strange house that is our own,
Where tricks of words are never said,
And mercy is as plain as bread
And honor is as hard as stone [31]

---

[31] "In Commemoration of Columbus Day." *Memoirs of Monsignor J.M. Kirwin,* George T. Elmendorf, Compiler. n. p.

Respect for the American Flag

While we are called to have a great respect for our Church, there should likewise be within each of us a great respect for the American flag. This can be easily drawn from American history books. One can recall the heroism of Washington and his troops at Valley Forge. Then there was the great triumph at Yorktown. Pakenham was stopped at the victorious Battle of New Orleans. One can again think of victory at Chapultepec and Vera Cruz in Mexico.

We can readily recall the Star Spangled Banner,

Long may it wave,
O'er the land of the free
And the home of the brave.

We have not been involved in entangling alliances. Rather, this country has been involved in prudent preparation. At that time in the history of this country, we were confident that no country would threaten the might and security of America. Rather, we are threatened by our own indifference, specifically to patriotic purposes and high ideals. We are inclined too much to material things. Our gravest danger comes from selfish indulgence and complacent optimism. As Fr. Kirwin stated, we "must show by our deeds that we prize honor above comfort and justice above gain and mercy above justice."

We are called to develop the virtue of patriotism. Repeated acts accomplish that. It is important to eternalize one's patriotic acts, whether it be on Flag Day, July 4th, Veterans' Day, or some other patriotic occasion. He referred back to the words of Sam Houston, the first President of the Republic of Texas:

> So long as that flag shall bear aloft its glittering stars, bearing them amidst the din of battle and waving them triumphantly above the storms of ocean, so long, I trust, shall the rights of American citizens be preserved safe and unimpaired and transmitted from one generation to another, till discord shall wreck the spheres, the grand march of time shall cease, and not one fragment of all creation be left to chafe on the bosom of eternity's waves. [32]

[33] Flags at Catholic Schools Honor Vets

Catholics Inform Yourselves

The occasion was the exemplification of the Fourth Degree Knights of Columbus, held in Houston on February 23, 1923. The

---

[32]"Respect for the American Flag," *Memoirs of Monsignor J.M. Kirwin,* George T. Elmendorf. Compiler. n.p.

[33] Catholiccourier.com.

Gospel centered around the Transfiguration. It was fitting that Msgr. Kirwn chose the passage, "Lord, it is good for us to be here" (Mt 17:4).

Msgr. Kirwin reminded the congregation of the setting for the Transfiguration, with Peter, James, and John, and of the appearance of Moses and Elijah. When they came down from the mountain, a demonized boy was brought to Christ. Members of the crowd stated that they had brought the child to the disciples, but the disciples were unable to cure him. Jesus referred to them as a faithless and perverse generation. Jesus cast the evil spirit out of the boy, and he was cured. The disciples then asked privately why they were not able to cure the boy. Jesus responded that it was because of their lack of faith.

This passage moved the Celebrant to the encyclical issued by Pope Pius XI, "On the Peace of Christ in the Kingdom of Christ." The Pontiff remarked that since the Great War or World War I, individuals have not found true peace. He pointed out that this tranquility is a great need of all mankind. This need also existed during the pontificate of Pope Benedict XV, his predecessor. A true and lasting reconciliation among all men is the ultimate goal.

The Pontiff called upon the prophets from the Old Testament: "We looked for peace and no good came: for a time of healing, and behold fear," (Jer. viii, 15) "for the time of healing, and behold trouble." (*Jer*. xiv, 19) "We looked for light, and behold darkness . . . we have looked for judgment, and there is none: for salvation, and it is far from us." (Isaiah lix, 9, 11)

Those who were enemies during World War I have put down their arms. However, there are future threats of war in the Middle

East and elsewhere. Nations at that time lived in a state of armed peace.

The name of the encyclical suggests the means by which peace may reign in the hearts of men. Pope Pius XI was referring to a spiritual peace. Specifically, the Pontiff was looking toward a peace which would penetrate the souls of individuals and therefore reopen the hearts of one another to a brotherly love. Certainly, this was the peace which Christ extended to His disciples (John 14:27). The peace of Christ is that which answers this description. The peace of Christ is called forth to reign in one's heart (Col 3:15).

The Pontiff went on to develop the presence of Christ's peace in the various spheres of our lives. Christ must be at the center of the family through the sacrament of Matrimony. Christ is called to be the foundation of the home. Christ is meant to be the center of our individual lives through Christian education. Pope Pius XI pleaded for the reign of law and order around the globe. He referred to a respect for authority within the home. Christ is called to be in the hearts of men by Christian charity and love. Ultimately, there is no peace within our hearts except through the reign of Christ.

Bearing in mind the fruit of the development of that peace of Christ, Pope Pius XI expressed his joy at the gathering of the International Eucharistic Congress and the observance of the Centenary of the Sacred Congregation for the Propagation of the Faith. Large numbers of prelates gathered for these anniversaries.

Members of the Knights of Columbus advanced toward a higher plane of service. Their gathering in Houston on February 23, 1923, was specifically intended to exemplify the Fourth Degree Knights of Columbus. The occasion called forth awareness of the Knights of

Columbus' ideals' development. Msgr. Kirwin thus stated that all are called to the practice of the virtue of charity.

There is much in this encyclical of Pope Pius XI that could not be developed in a short address. Msgr. Kirwin, therefore, called upon each knight to read the document and familiarize himself with its teaching. Catholics may find themselves subject to attack. These attacks may be more commonly addressed to the Fourth Degree Knights of Columbus. Yet all Catholics are called to know their faith and to be able to give an intelligent defense of it. One can best answer lies by living the truth and showing the world that his standard of faith and morals is the stainless banner of the crucified Christ. [34]

[35] Fourth Degree Knights of Columbus Insignia

Knights of Columbus Trip to Europe

Msgr. Kirwin toured France, Italy, England, and Ireland as part of a patriotic trip sponsored by the Knights of Columbus after the War. The purpose of the tour was to present Lafayette's statue to the

---

[34] "Catholics Inform Yourselves." *Memoirs of Monsignor J.M. Kirwin,* George T. Elmendorf, Compiler. n. p.

[35] Fourth Degree Knights of Columbus Insignia.

city of Metz. Msgr. Kirwin stated that the trip was an inspiration to everyone on the tour. He believed that the spirit of the French people inspired the Americans. The French people are saving their money. Before long, the franc will be worth what it used to be.

People may scoff at them and say that they have no religion, but that is a mistake. There is no denying the spirituality of the people as a whole. Every place they went, they received a cordial reception. It was a genuine and spontaneous welcome. The great sacrifices the people of France had endured during the war were most evident.

They also heard Marshal Petain's words about the sacrifices of the people of France. He noted Verdun along the Marne at Belleau Wood. Every man who heard Marshal Petain was given a new insight by way of the great sacrifices made by the soldiers of France. He referred to the brave defense of these French soldiers. In particular, Marshal Petain referred to the million men buried in the valley below. Not once did Marshal Petain use the personal pronoun. Those who heard him were stirred in their very hearts and souls by his words.

Msgr. Kirwin had the privilege of celebrating Mass at Lourdes and at several other historic cathedrals and churches during the guided tour. He served as chaplain of the Knights of Columbus party. Upon their return, the party presented him with a medal in appreciation of his services to them during the tour. When they did get back, approximately forty of his close friends gave him a little banquet at the Hotel Galvez as a kind of welcome home party.[36]

---

[36]"Knights of Columbus Trip to Europe," *Memoirs of Monsignor J.M. Kirwin,* George T. Elmendorf, Compiler. n.p.

Honors, the London Convention of Ad Clubs in 1924, and to Ireland in 1925

In 1920, Fr. Kirwin was decorated by the French government for his "splendid" services to the Allied cause during and after the War. Pope Pius XI gave him the title of Monsignor on June 24, 1922, for his extended and fruitful service to the Church. Bishop Byrne invested Msgr. Kirwin with the title of Domestic Prelate in December of 1922.[37]

Msgr. Kirwin accompanied approximately two hundred members of the Ad Club to London in 1924. From the French American baby who was going to visit his grandmother for the first time to Captain Blavier, master of the ship, everyone on board agreed that the most popular passenger was Msgr. Kirwin. Within ten days of their leaving Houston, the passengers knew each other, and Monsignor Kirwin knew them. He told jokes to the weeping wives who were leaving husbands behind. He organized an impromptu quartet. He was able to bring smiles to the faces of howling babies in short order. He celebrated Mass on Sunday mornings for the Catholics on board. He managed to have prayers said for all Protestants and Jews on board. After dinner, he started telling stories. One night, there was a storytelling contest. Msgr. Kirwin walked away with the prize. He himself told the yarn about

[37] Rev. Stephen P. Brown, "Monsignor James M. Kirwin, *Memoirs of Monsignor J.M. Kirwin,* George T. Elmendorf, Compiler. n.p.

a klansman, a Jew, and a Catholic. When someone found out his birthday was July 1, a huge cake was made for the occasion. [38]

It is believed that through the influence of Msgr. Kirwin, the Ad Club met in Houston in 1925. He was invited to Ireland in 1925 by Mr. Frank Flannigan, brother-in-law of the President of the Irish Free State. He made a notable speech in Dublin on "Conditions in Ireland" while there. He then went to Paris with the Ad Club to lay a wreath at the Tomb of the Unknown Soldier. A large crowd was there at the Tomb of the Unknown Soldier where he spoke, and a musician was playing a harp. Msgr. Kirwin praised the French for their tremendous aid during the American Revolution. It was the only speech given that day. It was reported in French and English newspapers and broadcast in other newspapers around the world. From there, he went to Rome and had an audience with Pope Pius XI. He returned by way of Genoa and Marseilles, then Ireland, and finally sailed back to America.

---

[38] "Kirwin Won Love of Delegates to London Ad Meet," *Houston Chronicle,* January, 1926.

AT THE WORLD-FAMOUS GROTTO—MONSIGNOR KIRWIN AT LOURDES, IN FRANCE

[39] Msgr. Kirwin is celebrating Mass at Lourdes as part of the Knights of Columbus Tour

[39] "At the World Famous Grotto-Monsignor Kirwin at Lourdes in France," *Memoirs of Monsignor J.M. Kirwin*, George T. Elmendorf, Compiler. n.p.

[40] Tomb of the Unknown Soldier in Paris
where Msgr. Kirwin spoke and laid a wreath.

[40] "Tomb of the Unknown Soldier, at which Msgr. Kirwin Spoke," Bonjour Paris.

Chapter Eight

Last Mass

Monsignor Kirwin maintained all of these positions even as his health began to fail in the summer of 1925. In the fall of that year, doctors told him he had high blood pressure and urged him to preserve his strength. He celebrated his last Mass on January 24, 1926. He asked the congregation at that Mass to pray for the repose of the soul of his dear friend, Fr. M. M. Meara of Columbus, Ohio. Fr. Meara had died exactly one year previous to that day.

It was a typical habit of Msgr. Kirwin is to take a nap on Sunday afternoon. According to the received narrative, on the afternoon of January 24, 1926, his housekeeper awoke him at 5:30 pm. Yet he wanted to sleep a bit longer. When he did not rise by 6:10 pm, she found him dead in bed, an apparent victim of a heart attack. The good Lord took him home in those final moments of sleep.

When the seminarians filed in for evening prayer and devotions, Fr. Rapp announced with trembling voice the loss of Msgr. Kirwin. The rosary followed. Few eyes were dry, few voices calm; the seminarians prayed that God would be merciful to him who had sacrificed his life to the Church and State. The seminarians were experiencing the loss of a beloved teacher. He had given fifteen years of his life to the seminarians. They held that forever in memory! While Msgr. Kirwin's task was done, the seminarians saw their role as just beginning, all for building the Church.

The very sudden death of Msgr. James Kirwin shocked seminarians, priests, bishops, parishioners, and family members. The common assumption was that the vicar general was in excellent health. Therefore, the high blood pressure must not have been commonly known. When the young seminarians reflected on the fifteen years of life Fr. Kirwin had given them, they saw him as a loving father. "In time of trouble or sadness, or mental or spiritual gloom, he bore us up, sought to console us in the magnanimity of spirit that so characterized him, lifted the load from our shoulders and placed it upon his own....His classes were always an hour of joy.... Every point was indelibly impressed upon the memory by some of the anecdotes for which he was widely known. Even though he ministered to a large parish, his teaching never suffered. As Bishop Joseph Lynch stated, he took great pride in his students. Further, he could hold his own in any company. He was known for being generous with others." [1]

A four-day funeral followed.

Funeral

The funeral service for Msgr. James Kirwin (1871-1926) was held at St. Mary's Cathedral in Galveston on Thursday, January 28, 1926. Before that service, the nephew of the deceased, Fr. J.M. Kirwin of Beaumont, offered a funeral Mass on Monday morning in

---

[1]Rev.Henry Brouilhet, A.B.," Seminarians' Tribute," and Edgar Odell Lovett, Ph.D. "Monsignor Kirwin as Educator," *"Eulogy by Bishop Lynch," Memoirs of Monsignor James M. Kirwin,* George T. Elmendorf, Compiler, n.p.

the Cathedral. Catholics, Protestants, and Jews filled the Cathedral for that Monday morning liturgy. A solemn requiem high Mass was offered for Msgr James Kirwin at Holy Rosary Church on Wednesday at 8:00 am in appreciation of the many kindnesses shown to the Dominican Order by Msgr Kirwin.

Merchants closed their stores during Msgr. 's funeral. James Kirwin.

Since Sunday night, members of the Third and Fourth Degree Knights of Columbus, the Catholic Knights of America, and the American Legion have kept a constant vigil around the coffin of Monsignor Kirwin. The recitation of the Office of the Dead preceded the Funeral Mass.

The celebrant for the Requiem Mass on Thursday at St. Mary's Cathedral was Bishop C.E. Byrne. Bishop Joseph Lynch, the Ordinary of the Diocese of Dallas, delivered the sermon. He chose the passage from St. Paul, 2 Tim 4:7-8: "I have competed well. I have finished the race; I have kept the faith. From now on, the crown of righteousness awaits me, which the Lord, the just Judge, will award to me on that day, and not only to me, but to all who have longed for His appearance."

Bishop Lynch referred to Msgr. 's life. Kirwin, as one rich in achievement yet golden in promise. When he referred to his life as scarcely beyond its meridian, it appears that he was emphasizing the achievement cut short and that of a great moral leader, as he described him. He was seen by many as an ardent scholar, a great patriot, a zealous priest, and a very loyal Vicar General. He was described as very interested in the spiritual development and moral standards of the people as a whole. He certainly was a promoter of the public order. He wished, as Christ stated in the Gospel, to render to Caesar the things that are Caesar's and to God the things that are God's. He treasured and often quoted from the Declaration of Independence and the Constitution of the United States. Like His Divine Master, he went about doing good for thirty years. That may have taken him into measures of wealth or poverty, the classroom or the distant battlefield. He was indeed grateful for the true sturdiness of his Catholic upbringing. There, he truly advanced in wisdom and grace. As the vicar general of his diocese for many years, he was most loyal to his bishop, whether past or present. He was justly proud of the achievements of his diocese's personnel. At the same time, everyone mourned the very sudden loss of Msgr. James Kirwn, Bishop Lynch, reminded the congregation that to whom much was given, much is expected. Thus, they were reminded to pray that as he ascended the throne of mercy, he would know the happy repose of his soul. [2]

After the funeral Mass and the clergy and honor guard had withdrawn, hundreds of people filed slowly past the coffin containing the remains of Msgr. Kirwin.

---

[2]"Funeral of Monsignor Kirwin Imposing Demonstration of Profound Esteem and Sorrow," *Southern Messenger*, February 4, 1926.

[3] Scenes at the Funeral of Monsignor Kirwin in Galveston, Texas

[4] Scenes at the Funeral of Monsignor Kirwin in Galveston, Texas

---

[3] "Scenes at the Funeral of Monsignor Kirwin in Galveston, Texas," *Memoirs of Monsignor J.M. Kirwin*, George T. Elmendorf, Compiler, n. p.

[4] Ibid.

Notification to the Kirwin Family in Ohio, followed by the burial

When someone from Galveston called Circleville, Ohio, to convey the news, the family did not have a phone in their home. The nephew of Msgr. Kirwin conveyed that his father had to go across the street to the flour mill around midnight. He came back in shock. His family decided not to tell his mother, Mrs. Kirwin, till the morning. Mrs. Kirwin called for his body to be sent home to Circleville, Ohio.

His nephew Fr. J.M. Kirwin, in addition to several other clergy and members of the diocese, led the train ride to his final resting place.[5] The body arrived late Saturday afternoon at the Kirwin home, which was covered with exquisite floral arrangements. Mrs. Kirwin, 87 years old, resigned to God's mercy, was bent over with grief, yet rejoiced that her son was brought home to her. He was laid out in the parlor of the family home. The expressions of sympathy from the city of Galveston and the tributes from the press deeply touched the family. An Irish wake followed.

Fr. James M Kirwin, nephew of the deceased Monsignor Kirwin, was the celebrant for the funeral Mass. It took place on Monday at 9:00 am at St. Joseph's Parish Church, which was filled to overflowing. School had been dismissed. Businesses had closed for the funeral. The Parish Choir sang the Requiem High Mass. The pastor of the parish for twenty-six years, Rev. J.S. Hanna, was deeply touched. He delivered the sermon. Bishop Francis Howard from

---

[5]Rapp, "Fr. James Kirwin, Soldier, Scholar, Priest."

Covington, Kentucky, plus several priests, were present in the sanctuary. Bishop Francis Howard from Covington, Kentucky, gave the final absolution at the Church—the remains of Msgr. James Kirwin was buried in St. Joseph's Parish Cemetery in Circleville, Ohio. Taps was played at the cemetery.[6]

Survivors of the Kirwin Family in Circleville, Ohio

Bishop Joseph Lynch pulled together the sentiments of so many who mourned such a sudden great loss, yet at peace that he arrived in his final resting place:

---

[6] Bob Giles, "Msgr. Kirwin: Soldier, Civilian," *Texas Catholic Herald* and Msgr. Kirwin Memorial Mass will be Celebrated January 24, 1997," *Texas Catholic Herald,* January 10, 1997, and "At Circleville, Ohio," *Memoirs of Monsignor J.M. Kirwin,* George T. Elmendorf, Compiler, n.p.

I shall come as a thief in the night when you least expect, with the Eucharistic kiss fresh upon his priestly lips, he folded about himself his mantle to appear no more to mortal eye, except in the majesty of death, in which we now behold him.

May the angels of God, whom you have so faithfully served, receive you into paradise, and may you take your place in the company of the Immaculate Lamb and the Immaculate Mother to enjoy peace and refreshment and wave the palm of victory that you have so richly merited. May your great soul rest in peace. Plaque at the beginning of the book of memoirs:

Rt Rev. Msgr. James M. Kirwin, V.G.
Soldier, Scholar, Priest
Born July 1, 1872, ordained June 19, 1895
Died January 24, 1926
From yonder altar after sabbath hymn
Retreating gently, sweetly, with thy host.
To thine own chamber there communing still
True to him, thy god, didst give up thy soul
In humble resignation to his will.
r.i.p.

Chapter Nine

Accomplishments of and Tributes to Monsignor James Kirwin

Looking Back

It all began for Fr. James Kirwin in the Galveston diocese when the previous Bishop, Bishop Nicholas Gallagher, was having some difficulty in communication with various members of the diocese, whether the Ursuline Sisters in Galveston who wished to keep their chapel open to the public against the desires of Bishop Gallagher, or the newly arrived foreign born parishioners who were looking for a pastor who spoke their language as English was still a foreign tongue, to the many other complaints from parishioners who made the episcopate of Bishop Nicholas Gallagher a difficult road. The then-current archbishop of New Orleans, Archbishop Francis Joseph Janssens, recommended to Bishop Gallagher that he find a priest who could take on the communications aspect of the episcopal administration. At the same time, Bishop Gallagher would continue his strictly administrative role. Since Bishop Gallagher came from Ohio, he was familiar with Fr. James Kirwin[1]

[1] Fr. James Vanderholt, "Friend to All, Ecumenist, Theologian, Administrator, Chaplain, Civil Leader, Fr. James Martin Kirwin," *The Catholic Herald,* n.d.

Bishop Gallagher had done some recruiting in his old stomping grounds. There, he had to learn of James Kirwin. The seminarian had attended St. Joseph's College in Bardstown, Kentucky, and then went on to receive his bachelor's degree from St. Mary's College in Lebanon, Kentucky, in 1894. He then attended Mount St. Mary's of the West Seminary in Cincinnati. He studied Graduate Theology there. This was part of his preparation for future ministry in the diocese of Galveston. While there, he and another seminarian wrote and published a history of that Seminary. The work was highly regarded then and today, even by Msgr. John Tracy Ellis. [2]

Kirwin was ordained to the priesthood on June 15, 1895, by Archbishop William Elder of Cincinnati. Bishop Gallagher sent Kirwin to Catholic University for one year. Fr. J.J. Keane, president of Catholic University, wrote: "I cannot tell you how sorry we are at not receiving back Fr. Kirwin this year. He is, in many respects, a model student, just the kind of man we like to have here." [3]

Bishop Gallagher summoned Fr. Kirwin to Galveston on August 15, 1896. [4] He then became rector of the Cathedral and a leader within the Galveston diocese in urging individuals to overcome the yellow fever epidemic by taking on proper sanitary regulations. As a result, the city never had to face that threat to life again. [5]

---

[2] Ibid.

[3] Ibid.

[4] Don Rapp,'62, "Fr. James Kirwin, Soldier, Scholar, Priest," *The Kirwinite,*29:2, January 30, 1962.

[5] Vanderholt, "Friend to All, Ecumenist, Theologian, Administrator, Chaplain, Civil Leader, Fr. James Martin Kirwin."

The United States went to war with Spain in 1898. The people of Galveston decided to form a volunteer regiment. Fr. Kirwin was a great help in this endeavor due to his patriotic speeches. The men, therefore, asked him to be their chaplain. The War Department enthusiastically accepted their choice and promoted him to the rank of Captain. He served two years and then received an Honorable Discharge. Years later, in 1915, he served as a Catholic chaplain with the Fourth Infantry on the Mexican Border. During World War I, he was the principal speaker for the Liberty Loan Drives in Galveston. He also worked with the Red Cross to minister to the Army camps. [6]

The 1900 storm was a much greater threat to the city than the yellow fever epidemic. Bishop Gallagher himself did not believe survival would follow. Fr. Kirwin set up the Central Relief Committee to provide the basic needs of food and clothing for those who survived the storm and, likewise, those who were caring for the injured. Over six thousand people were found dead. Fr. Kirwin issued the order placing the city under martial law. This, in turn, saved the city from vandalism. With so many Galvestonians having expired in the storm, there was no way of burying the bodies. Likewise, burying the bodies at sea failed as the sea brought the bodies back to shore. There was no other way than cremation. It was a necessary public health measure. The stench from what took place lingered in the city for some time, but again, it was the only recourse.

---

[6] Rapp, "Fr. James Kirwin, Soldier, Scholar, Priest," Memorial Mass in Honor of Msgr. James J. Kirwin," *The Texas Catholic Herald,* January 12, 1979, and Bob Giles, "Msgr. Kirwin: For 30 Years Trudged Highways of Southland," *The Texas Catholic Herald,* February 2, 1979.

272F Fr. Kirwin initiated plans for a seawall with an opening prayer at the laying of the cornerstone in 1902. He also officiated at the closing exercises in 1905, when the commemorative monuments were unveiled. [7]

Fr. Kirwin rescued several people from blazing buildings in 1901. Unfortunately, he permanently injured his eyes in the process. As a result of the fire, the city had to increase its water supply and strengthen fire department training. The Fire Department, in appreciation of Fr. Kirwin's heroism, presented the prelate with a gold medal. [8]

In 1903, Bishop Gallagher selected Fr. Kirwin as the Diocesan Director for the Propagation of the Faith. [9]

A dock workers' strike broke out four years later, in 1907. Unfortunately, freight stacked up. Strike breakers were called in. Traffic in the harbor was at a standstill. The citizens asked Fr. Kirwin to intervene. He went to the strikers, met with them, and then met with the owners. Gradually, each side gave in on various points, to the satisfaction of both. [10]

Galveston had a reputation of being an "open city" in 1909. Saloons were posing as corner grocery stores and had established themselves in neighborhoods. The city charter could not change this. Thus, Fr. Kirwin led a group to the state legislature to pass a bill eliminating the neighborhood saloons. Many of the state legislators

---

[7] Rapp, "Fr. James Kirwin, Soldier, Scholar, Priest."

[8] Ibid.

[9] Vanderholt, "Friend to All, Ecumenist, Theologian, Administrator, Chaplain, Civil Leader, Fr. James Martin Kirwin."

[10] Ibid.

did not like the bill that was passed. As a result, neighborhood saloons were banished. However, when the legislation was passed, Fr. Kirwin was credited with the victory and made no enemies in the process. [11]

The Basilians left St. Mary's Seminary on June 15, 1911, as a result of a disagreement between Bishop Gallagher and the Order. [12] Gallagher was delighted that this allowed the bishop to choose his own men, the first of which was Fr. Kirwin as President. This took place in 1911. The train ride between Galveston and La Porte allowed Kirwin to carry out duties at the Cathedral and the Seminary. He taught in the classroom Theology, Scripture, Biblical Studies, Latin, Spanish, and the Catechism. It was not uncommon for the President to take on a student seminarian in the evening who was behind in a particular subject. While he taught classes, he also taught by example. As any seminarian would testify, he was an inspiration to them. [13] He had a way of mixing a bit of frivolity with wise counsel. He was generous in his judgment of others. [14]

Bishop Gallagher appointed Kirwin as Vicar General in 1911. This position required knowledge of canon law. He was reappointed by Bishop Byrne and maintained that role until his passing. During these years, he was recognized as "The Fighting Parson." [15]He was

---

[11] Ibid.

[12] The Basilian provincial stated the religious order was overextended, yet in fact Bishop Gallagher was not pleased with the leadership at the Seminary and demanded a change. See Raphael O'Laughlin, CSB, *Basilian Leaders from Texas* (Houston, Texas, Wing Press, 1991), 28.

[13] Rapp, "Fr. James Kirwin, Soldier, Scholar, Priest."

[14] Edgar Odell Lovett, Ph.D., "Monsignor Kirwin as an Educator."

[15] Rapp, "Fr. James Kirwin, Soldier, Scholar, Priest."

recognized for his role in the Liberty Loan Drive during the Great War. In the year 1920, the French government decorated Fr. Kirwin for his service to the Allied cause during and after World War I.

Pope Pius XI extended to him the ecclesiastical title of Monsignor on June 24, 1922. [16] As noted earlier, this recognition of his work for the Church was twenty years overdue. This delay was caused by an unkind correspondence sent to Rome regarding his decision to burn bodies after the 1900 storm.

Msgr. Kirwin was known as an unequal orator within and beyond the diocese. Bishop Gallagher chose him early on, after his arrival, to deliver the sermon or address at whatever function was followed by the bishop's blessing. Their teamwork became known all over the diocese. Notre Dame University awarded Msgr. Kirwin received the degree of Doctor of Laws in June 1923. As previously noted, Msgr. Kirwin was also quite outspoken against the Ku Klux Klan.

On a civilian level, Fr. Kirwin was recognized as "Big Jim." The story goes that one Saturday night in Galveston, before prohibition, there was a barroom brawl in a saloon along the Galveston wharf. Knives and guns were drawn. The police were called. The police chief, Chief William Henry Perrett, knew that uniformed officers could easily inflame the situation. To prevent bloodshed, he rode down to the Cathedral rectory and explained the situation to Fr. Kirwin. They were on their way in a flash. Fr. Kirwin swung the doors of the barroom open. Suddenly, there was quiet. "Boys," he forcefully admonished, "It's getting pretty late. Some of you would

---

[16] Ibid.

want to be on time for the 6:00 am Mass. What do you say, let's call it a day?" The party was over. There was no bloodshed. Fr. Kirwin knew his fellow man. [17]

Group of Teaching Staff and Student Body at
St. Mary's Seminary, La Porte, Texas

[17] Bob Giles, "Big Jim: Msgr. Kirwin: Soldier, Civilian," *The Catholic Herald,* n.d.

Last Seminary Faculty under Monsignor Kirwin. Father G. Elmendorf, compiler of Memoirs. Second from Right, Second Row

Tributes flowed in from the seminary, the parish, the diocese, the state, and the nation. Odin High School was closed, and a new Catholic high school, Kirwin High School, opened in its place.

[18] Kirwin High School

The diocese of Galveston purchased the residence of the late Col. William L. Moody, Sr., in 1927. It was converted into a high school for boys and named in honor of Msgr. James Kirwin. The Dominican and Ursuline Sisters operated the school until 1931, when the Brothers of the Christian School took over. By 1942, the high school for boys needed a more modern facility, which was built on the same site at 23rd Street, between Avenues M and N. In 1961, an addition to the building included a new gym and cafetorium.

The Fr. Kirwin Memorial

Scarcely six weeks after his passing, a committee consisting of Rev. I.J. Reicher, Rev. M.S. Chataignon, and Bayliss E. Harris

---

[18] Courtesy of Galveston and Texas History Center, Rosenberg Library.

originated the idea of a memorial in honor of Monsignor James M. Kirwin. Catholics and non-Catholics alike wished to start a fund for a memorial. It was believed there were enough friends of Msgr. Kirwin to make the memorial a reality. A fund of $200,000.00 was necessary to carry out the plan. This could be done through subscription contributions or cash. A $5,000 subscription had already been made. The structure would be referred to as the Fr. Kirwin Memorial. [19]

The Fr. Kirwin Memorial was dedicated in May, 1928.

The Fr. Kirwin Memorial was used by the Seminarians in La Porte as their Chapel until a new Seminary was built for them on Memorial Drive in Houston. in 1954. This Chapel was shared by the

---

[19] "Galveston Citizens Sponsor Fine Memorial to Msgr. Kirwin," *Southern Messenger*, March 4, 1926.

Catholics living in the LaPorte, Texas area. Today, it is recognized as St. Mary's Parish in the Galveston-Houston archdiocese.

Rt Rev. Msgr. James M. Kirwin, V.G.

Soldier, Scholar, Priest
Born July 1, 1872, ordained June 19, 1895
Died January 24, 1926
From yonder altar after sabbath hymn
Retreating gently, sweetly, with thy host.
To thine own chamber there communing still
True to him, thy god, didst give up thy soul
In humble resignation to his will.
r.i.p. [20]

[20] From Cover and Plaque of *Memoirs of Monsignor J.M. Kirwin.*

Bibliography

Books and Portions of Books

"Accomplishments of and Tributes to Monsignor James Kirwin." George T. Elmendorf, Compiler. *Memoirs of Monsignor J.M. Kirwin.*

"At the World Famous Grotto-Monsignor Kirwin at Lourdes in France." George T. Elmendorf, Compiler. *Memoirs of Monsignor J.M. Kirwin.*

"Birthplace of Fr. Kirwin in Circleville, Ohio." George T. Elmendorf, Compiler. *Memoirs of Monsignor J.M. Kirwin.*

Brown, Stephen P. "Monsignor James M. Kirwin." George T. Elmendorf, Compiler. *Memoirs of Monsignor J.M. Kirwin.*

Castañeda, Carlos. *Our Catholic Heritage in Texas, 1836-1950.* v. 7 Austin, Texas: Von Boeckmann-Jones, 1958.

"Catholics Inform Yourselves." George T. Elmendorf, Compiler. *Memoirs of Monsignor J.M. Kirwin.*

"The Christian Soldier." George T. Elmendorf, Compiler. *Memoirs of Monsignor J.M. Kirwin.*

Diamond Jubilee of the Diocese of Galveston and St. Mary's Cathedral (1847-1922). Compiled by the Priests of the Diocese.

*Diocese of Galveston-Houston Sesquicentennial, 1847-1997.*Foreword by Bishop Joseph A. Fiorenza, Bishop of Galveston. Dallas, TX: Taylor Publishing Co., 1997.

Elmendorf, George T., Compiler. *Memoirs of Monsignor J.M. Kirwin.*

"Fr. James Martin Kirwin. Chaplain, First US Volunteer Regiment, Spanish-American War."

George T. Elmendorf, Compiler. *Memoirs of Monsignor J.M. Kirwin.*

Fr. James Kirwin, "No Place for Prejudice." George T. Elmendorf, Compiler. *Memoirs of Monsignor J.M. Kirwin.*

"Fr. Kirwin as Domestic Prelate." George T. Elmendorf, Compiler. *Memoirs of Monsignor J.M. Kirwin.*

"Fr. Meara and Fr. Kirwin," George T. Elmendorf, Compiler. *Memoirs of Monsignor J.M. Kirwin.*

"Funeral and Burial." George T. Elmendorf, Compiler. *Memoirs of Monsignor J.M. Kirwin.*

Hackett, O.P., Sr. Shelia. *Dominican Women in Texas, from Ohio to Galveston and Beyond.* Houston, TX: Sacred Heart Convent. 1986.

"Hearers and Doers of the Word." George T. Elmendorf, Compiler. *Memoirs of Monsignor J.M. Kirwin.*

Hegarty, CCVI, Sr. Loyola. *Serving with Gladness. The Origin of the Congregation of the Sisters of Charity of the Incarnate Word, Houston, Texas.* Houston, TX: Bruce Publishing Company in Cooperation with the Sisters of Charity of the Incarnate Word, Houston, Texas. 1967.

"In Commemoration of Columbus Day." George T. Elmendorf, Compiler. *Memoirs of Monsignor J.M. Kirwin.*

"Ireland's Patron Saint." George T. Elmendorf, Compiler. *Memoirs of Monsignor J.M. Kirwin.*

"James M Kirwin as a Young Man." George T. Elmendorf, Compiler. *Memoirs of Monsignor J.M. Kirwin.*

Kauffman, Christopher. "McGivney, Michael J. (1852-1890)." *The Encyclopedia of American Catholic History.* Michael Glazier and Thomas J. Shelley. Collegeville, Minnesota: A Michael Glazier Book. The Liturgical Press. 1997.

"The Kirwin Family of Circleville, Ohio." George T. Elmendorf, Compiler. *Memoirs of Monsignor J.M. Kirwin.*

Kirwin, Fr. James. "Be Slow to Speak." George T. Elmendorf, Compiler. *Memoirs of Monsignor J.M. Kirwin.*

Kirwin, Fr. James. "No Place for Prejudice." George T. Elmendorf, Compiler. *Memoirs of Monsignor J.M. Kirwin.*

"Knights of Columbus Trip to Europe." George T. Elmendorf, Compiler. *Memoirs of Monsignor J.M. Kirwin.*

"Last Mass." George T. Elmendorf, Compiler. *Memoirs of Monsignor J.M. Kirwin.*

"The Loaves and the Fish." George T. Elmendorf, Compiler. *Memoirs of Monsignor J.M. Kirwin.*

"London Convention of Ad Clubs in 1924, to Ireland in 1925." George T. Elmendorf, Compiler. *Memoirs of Monsignor J.M. Kirwin.*

"Monsignor James Kirwin." George T. Elmendorf, Compiler. *Memoirs of Monsignor J.M. Kirwin.*

Moore, James Talmadge. *Acts of Faith: The Catholic Church in Texas 1900-1950.* College Station: Texas A & M University Press. 2002.

"My Grace Is Sufficient for You." George T. Elmendorf, Compiler. *Memoirs of Monsignor J.M. Kirwin.*

Oberste, William H. *Knights of Columbus in Texas 1902-1952.* Austin, TX: Von Boeckmann-Jones Company, 1951.

O'Neill, Michael. "Blessed Michael McGivney, Parish Priest and Founder of the Knights of Columbus," *They Might Be Saints on the Path to Sainthood in America.* Irondale, Alabama. EWTN Publishing, Inc., 2021.

"Persecution of the French Church." George T. Elmendorf, Compiler. *Memoirs of Monsignor J.M. Kirwin.*

"Respect for the American Flag." George T. Elmendorf, Compiler. *Memoirs of Monsignor J.M. Kirwin.*

"Sacred Heart Church." George T. Elmendorf, Compiler. *Memoirs of Monsignor J.M. Kirwin.*

"Self-Denial, Looking at the Essence of Religion." George T Elmendorf. Compiler. *Memoirs of Monsignor J.M. Kirwin.*

"The Storm of 1900." George T Elmendorf, Compiler. *Memoirs of Monsignor J.M. Kirwin.*

"Strength Gained through Prayer." George T. Elmendorf, Compiler. *Memoirs of Monsignor J.M. Kirwin.*

"Survivors of the Kirwin Family." George T. Elmendorf, Compiler. *Memoirs of Monsignor J.M. Kirwin.*

"The Transfiguration." George T. Elmendorf, Compiler. *Memoirs of Monsignor J.M. Kirwin.*

"Thy Sins Are Forgiven Thee (Mt 9:2)." George T. Elmendorf, Compiler. *Memoirs of Monsignor J.M. Kirwin.*

"Victory after World War I." George T. Elmendorf, Compiler. *Memoirs of Monsignor J.M. Kirwin.*

Newspapers

"'Ancient Order of Hibernians.'– Ku Klux Klan Denounced by Board of Directors.'" *The Southern Messenger.* August 17, 1922.

"Anti-Klan Bill Passed by Lower Illinois House." *The Southern Messenger.* March 3, 1923.

"Anti-Klan Bill Passed in Nebraska." *The Southern Messenger.* February 1, 1923.

"Anti-Saloon League Workers Address Large Crowds Here." *The Galveston Daily News.* Monday, March 31, 1918.

"The Battle Royal Is On – Kleagle of Texas Klan Is 'Fired' by Evans." *The Southern Messenger.* June 23, 1923.

"Bigotry in Atlanta, Press Denounces Educational Commissioner's Intolerance." *The Southern Messenger.* May 4, 1922.

"Brutal Outrage on a Catholic Priest." *The Southern Messenger.* March 16, 1922.

"Catholic War Records Essential to Refute False Statements of the Ku Klux Klan." *Southern Messenger.* November 2, 1922.

"Chicago's Campaign against the Ku Klux – Publication of Members' Names Leads to Resignations." *The Southern Messenger.* October 12, 1922.

"Cornerstone Laid of Newman Hall, Austin, Home for Catholic Women Students at State University, to be Conducted by Dominican Sisters. History and Scope of the Work Outlined by Very Rev. J.M. Kirwin in Eloquent Address." *The Southern Messenger.* March 14, 1918.

"Forty-Five Men Implicated in Mer Rouge Murder. Authorities Said to be in Possession of Details of Kidnapping and Killing." *The Southern Messenger.* January 4, 1923.

"Fr. Duffy Addresses Rainbow Veterans-Despite Klan Protest." *The Southern Messenger.* August 9, 1923.

"Funeral of Monsignor Kirwin Imposing Demonstration of Profound Esteem and Sorrow." *The Southern Messenger.* February 4, 1926.

"Galveston Citizens Sponsor Fine Memorial to Msgr. Kirwin." *The Southern Messenger.* March 4, 1926.

Giles, Bob. "Msgr. Kirwin Memorial Mass Will Be Celebrated January 24, 1997," *Texas Catholic Herald,* January 10, 1997.

Giles, Bob. "Msgr. Kirwin: Soldier, Civilian." *Texas Catholic Herald.* January 10, 1997.

"Governor Allen Not Converted by Dr. Evans-Determined to Drive Klan Out of Kansas." *The Southern Messenger.* December 28, 1922.

"Kirwin Won Love of Delegates to London Ad Meet." *Houston Chronicle.* January, 1926.

"Klan Criminals Should Be Punished, Governor Parker Says." *The Southern Messenger.* July 5, 1923.

"Klan Denounced by Labor Federation, Convention Declares Kluxers Menace to Government." *The Southern Messenger.* October 11, 1923.

"Klan's Candidates in Baton Rouge Lose Nominations." *The Southern Messenger.* August 3, 1922.

"Klan Ousts Many Catholics from School Positions." *The Southern Messenger*. July 24, 1924.

"Klan to be Investigated: Federal and Municipal Authorities to Look into the Masked Organization." *Southern Messenger*. October 6, 1921.

"Klansmen Interrupt Religious Services-Intruders Rebuked by Minister." *The Southern Messenger*. July 26, 1923

"Knights of Columbus." *The Southern Messenger*. February 22, 1923.

"Ku Klux Klan Adopts New Tactics." *The Southern Messenger*. August 14, 1924.

"Ku Klux Klan Scathingly Denounced by Oliver Allstorm, Former Klan Lecturer Asserts Hooded Organization Rapidly Disintegrating in Texas." *Southern Messenger*. November 1, 1923.

"Ku Klux Outbreak at Wallis, Texas." *Southern Messenger*. July 7, 1921.

"Ku Klux Pastor Scored by Baptists-Ministers.' Conference Condemns Acts of Dr. C.A. Ridley." *The Southern Messenger*. June 21, 1923.

"Ku Klux Attempt to Invade American Army 'No Divided Allegiance Will be Permitted,' Says Chairman of Senate Committee on Military Affairs.'" *The Southern Messenger*. August 24, 1922.

"Ku Klux Klan Strongly Denounced by Judge Reynolds of Dallas, 'Life' Member of Klan." *The Southern Messenger*. May 31, 1923.

"Lafayette Klan Disbands." *The Southern Messenger*. April 12, 1923.

"League of Protestant Women Declines to Affiliate with the Ku Klux Klan." *The Southern Messenger*. June 21, 1923.

"Masons Outlaw Klan in Pennsylvania. Opposed to Organization. Forbid Use of Masonic Property." *The Southern Messenger.* January 4, 1923.

McGreal, P.D. "Ku Klux Klan Scathingly Denounced by Oliver Allstrom, Former Klan Lecturer Asserts Hooded Organization Rapidly Disintegrating in Texas." *The Southern Messenger.* November 1, 1923.

McGreal, P.L. "Truth Society A Big Factor in Thwarting Revival of the Klan in Outlying Districts." *The Southern Messenger.* July 2, 1925.

"Membership Peddlers Take Special Pledge to Defend Klan Emperor." *The Galveston Daily News.* September 9, 1921.

"Methodist Minister Branded with 'KKK' After Pulpit Sermon." *The Southern Messenger."* July 24, 1924.

"Monsignor Gleissner's Diamond Jubilee to the Priesthood Celebrated." *The Southern Messenger.* December 1, 1949.

"Only Duty of Klan Is to Disband at Once – Says *Wall Street Journal* in Recent Editorial." *The Southern Messenger,* October 11, 1923.

"Original K.K.K. Worked for Order." *The Galveston Daily News.* Sunday, July 3, 1921.

Patrick Scanlan. K.S.C, "Man of the Past: Former Grand Dragon of the K.K.K." *Brooklyn* Tablet, January 24, 1957.

"President Coolidge Lauds Work of A.O.H. in Letter." *The Southern Messenger.* July 30, 1925.

"Protestants Will Fight the Ku Klux Klan – To Maintain American Institutions and Principles As Established 140 Years Ago." *The Southern Messenger.* August 31, 1922.

Rapp,'62, Don. "Fr. James Kirwin, Soldier, Scholar, Priest." *The Kirwinite.*29:2. January 30, 1962.

Rapp, Don. "Memorial Mass in Honor of Msgr. James J. Kirwin." *The Texas Catholic Herald.* January 12, 1979.

"The Real Menace of the Klan." *The Southern Messenger.* January 4, 1923.

"Religious Liberty at Stake." *The Southern Messenger.* August 10, 1922

"Speed Final Decision on Dry Measures." *San Antonio Light*, Saturday. March 16, 1918.

"Texas Ku Klux Klan Aims to Abolish Private and Parochial Schools and Convents of the Good Shepherd." *Southern Messenger.* January 4, 1923.

"Threat to Destroy a Catholic Church in Beaumont, Texas." *The Southern Messenger.* March 23, 1922

"Twenty-Four Klansmen Face Charges of Murder after Lilly Riot." *The Southern Messenger.* April 17, 1924.

"2,800,000 Klansmen withdraw from Organization – Members Express Dissatisfaction of Present Administration." *The Southern Messenger.* January 10, 1924.

Vanderholt, Fr. James. "Friend to All, Ecumenist, Theologian, Administrator, Chaplain, Civil Leader. Fr. James Martin Kirwin." *The Catholic Herald.* n.d.

"Violence Feared if Klan Lawlessness Exposed-Hearing Opens to Probe Killings in Mer Rouge." *The Southern Messenger.* January 11, 1923.

"Virginia Protestants Condemn the Kidnapping of Father V.D. Warren." *The Southern Messenger.* September 23, 1926.

"Wearing Robes of Klan Held Criminal: Texas Klansman Sentenced to Two Years' Imprisonment." *The Southern Messenger*. October 18, 1923.

Websites

"Archbishop Francis Janssens." St. Louis Cathedral.

Barton, Clara, and Peak, Don. "A Story of the Red Cross." Galveston County Historical Museum and the Rosenberg Library.

"Bishop Claude Dubuis." Castroville Area Chamber of Commerce.

"Blessed Sacrament Visits." Catholiccurrent.org.

"Brenham Ku Klux Klan Disbands on Motion of Barney Parker." Circular Distributed over Washington County, Texas.

"Building of the Seawall." Visit Galveston.com.

"Castaneda. Dr. Carlos." Humanities, Texas.

Catholic Center in College Station. "Aggie Land." Theeagle.com.

"Clara Barton (1821-1912). Foundress of the American Red Cross." Women's History.org.

"Claude Dubuis." Castroville Area Chamber of Commerce.

"Dr. Carlos Castaneda." Humanities, Texas.

"Emblem of the Knights of Columbus." 110 Knights of Columbus ideas.

"Flags at Catholic School Honor Veterans." Catholiccourier.com.

"A Flyer for Ku Klux Klan Day at the State Fair of Texas."

"Fourth Degree Knights of Columbus Insignia."

"Freedmen's Bureau Acts of 1865 and 1866." United States Senate.

"Fr. James A. Coyle, (1873-1921), Irish Priest Who Stood Up to the Klan." Find a Grave.com.

"Fr. Michael McGivney. Founder of the Knights of Columbus." Catholictradition.org.

Galveston County Historical Museum.

Galveston Seawall, Galveston and Texas History Center.

"General John J. Pershing, (1860-1948), Black Jack, Mexican Expedition, American Expeditionary Force." Pbs.org.

"God is faithful, and He will not let you be tested beyond your strength." 1 Cor 10:13. Pinterest.com.

Gonzalez, Anibal A. "Kirwin, James Martin," *Handbook of Texas Online*. https://tshaonline.org/handbook/entries/kirwin-james-martin. Published by the Texas State Historical Association.

"The Good Samaritan." *The Central Minnesota Catholic.*

"Hearers of the Word vs Doers of the Word." Catholic Sunday Scripture. Linked in.com.

Henry Wadsworth Longfellow. "Evangeline—A Tale of Acadie 1847." Maine Historical Society. www.hwlongfellow.org.

"His Holiness Pope Leo XIII." Denver Register.Org.

"Historical Marker, St. Mary's Cathedral, Galveston." Historical Marker Database.

"The Home Protective League." Galveston, TX, v. 1, No. 3. January 29, 1909.

"Office of the Historian, Foreign Service Institute, United States Department of State."

"Home Protective League, January 29, 1909." Courtesy of Rosenberg Library.

"I Am the Living Bread that came down from heaven. Whoever eats this bread will live forever." John 6:51. Catholiccurrent.org.

Interior of Sacred Heart Church, Galveston, Holyfamilygb.com.

Jolly, Amber and Ted Banks. "Dallas Klan No. 66," *Handbook of Texas Online.* https://www.tshaonline.org/handbook/entries/dallas-ku-klux-klan-no-66.

"Kirwin and the Klan." Holdings of Rosenberg Library. Galveston, TX.

Knights of Columbus Logo.

Knights of Columbus. Msgr. George A. Wilhelm Assembly. #1094.

Knights of Columbus. Our History.org.

Knights of Columbus. Msgr. George A. Wilhelm Assembly. #1094.

"The Martyrs of Arras." Daughters-of-Charity.com.

Newman Hall. Austin, TX. Austinpostcard.com.

"New York Newspapers Warn Klansmen Not to Attempt to Defy Law." *The Southern Messenger.* June 7, 1923.

Patron Saints of the Military, Catholictradition.Org.

Peak, Don and Clara Barton. "A Story of the Red Cross." Courtesy of the Rosenberg Library.

"Prayer for the Faithful by St. Patrick." Share Catholic.com.

"Remembering James Coyle: The Irish Priest the Ku Klux Klan Killed." James Wilson@JamesWilson.1919.

"Ring it again, Second Liberty Loan of 1917." Courtesy of the Library of Congress.

"Rt. Rev. Msgr. J.M. Kirwin, Vicar General of Galveston," *The Southern Messenger.* December 14, 1922. Fr. Anton J. Frank. Anniversary Death of Monsignor James M. Kirwin at Mass in Annunciation Church. Houston, Texas. Thursday, January 24, 1980. sponsored by Monsignor Kirwin Post Catholic War Veterans.

"Sacred Heart Church. Galveston." Holyfamilygb.com.

Stanthonyofsaranac.org.

Stmaryoticandhoc.org.

Stevens, Christina Strommen. "The Historical Sacred Heart Church in Galveston, Texas. A True Beauty of Our Time."

"St. Joseph's Infirmary. Houston, Texas." Houston Time Portal.net.

"St. Mary's Infirmary after the Storm." Courtesy of Rosenberg Library.

"St. Mary's Infirmary before the 1900 Storm." Courtesy of Rosenberg Library.

"St. Thomas Aquinas, O.P., 1225-1274." Catholic.org.

"Tomb of the Unknown Soldier.,Paris at which Msgr. Kirwin Spoke." Bonjour Paris.

"The Transfiguration, Artist: Raffaello Sanzioda Urbino known as Raphael. Ncregister.com.

"Ursuline Academy before the Storm." Courtesy Rosenberg Library.

"Ursuline Academy after the Storm." Courtesy of Rosenberg Library.

Vanderholt, James F. "Dufal, Pierre." *Handbook of Texas Online.* https://www.tshaonline.org/handbook/entries/dufal-pierre.

"You Are Forgiven." Stmaryoticandhoc.Org.

Index

www.ingramcontent.com/pod-product-compliance
Lightning Source LLC
LaVergne TN
LVHW020507100826
845148LV00003B/722

9798888705483